To Dsc
with
from .

A Good Life—At Any Price

Human life is under the special protection of God because each person

> however lowly or exalted,
> however sick and suffering,
> however useless or important,
> whether born or unborn,
> however fatally ill or abounding in health

… bears in himself the breath of God, each one is in the image of God.

Pope Emeritus Benedict

Halt at the cross-roads, look well, and ask yourselves which path it was that stood you in good stead long ago. That path follow, and you shall find rest for your souls.

Jeremiah 6:16

A Good Life—at Any Price

New Threats to Human Life in Our Times

Anita Dowsing

GRACEWING

First published in England in 2020
by
Gracewing
2 Southern Avenue
Leominster
Herefordshire HR6 0QF
United Kingdom
www.gracewing.co.uk

ISBN 978 085244 961 5

Typeset by Gracewing

Cover design by Bernardita Peña Hurtado

CONTENTS

PREFACE

T HE IDEA FOR the present book began to take shape while I was writing my previous one, *The Gift of Self in Marriage*, on the meaning of the act of love in marriage.[1] There I touched on embryo wastage and abortion, but did not treat these topics in any depth. I therefore knew that there was material for a further book on the threat to human beings at the early stages of life. However, I soon realised that this is not the only new threat to life in our times; the lives of handicapped or seriously ill adults are also at risk. Therefore life both at its beginning and end is under threat for the sake of a perceived good life; there is a third group, however, consisting of the many lives threatened by terrorism for the sake of what the terrorist believes to be a better existence. With the exception of embryo destruction, these threats have probably always existed in some form, but their rapid increase in our times is a new phenomenon. In order to counteract the many threats to life, it is necessary to care for every human life, however vulnerable or handicapped. In the final chapters of the book, I therefore discuss ways of protecting human beings, because this is the only path to a good life for everyone. A book on these topics for the general reader seemed very necessary, as, to my knowledge, no such work exists at present.

I need to say a word about the expression 'a good life', because it will mean different things to different people. When I use this phrase, I mean a life lived in truth, according to how things really are rather than how I would like them to be. This is how Christ lived his life. In practical terms, this could mean that, if I see a child on the other side of the road who has obviously just fallen off his bike, then I do not pass by, pretending not to have seen him, but I cross the road and offer to help. If I do that, then I am acting according to the mind of Christ; I am living in truth.

In our pluralistic society there is no generally accepted religious truth, as was the case until recently, at least in the West. This development has had consequences for all of us, because different opinions about religion and ethics are not just about theory, but about how people act. As more and more individuals take it for granted that certain categories of human beings, notably the embryo and the child in the womb, do not have an automatic right to life, others are influenced by them, so that practices like embryo destruction and abortion are no longer questioned. A similar slide towards the destruction of life is taking place in relation to sick and handicapped people. Legislation in an increasing number of countries has now been changed to accommodate this shift. Already far more lives have been lost through these practices than were killed in the Second World War. Outside the law, a growing number of lives are lost due to terrorist attacks.

Over against these developments, the right to life of every individual has consistently been upheld by many religions, notably the Catholic Church, whose teaching forms a major part of this book. In secular terms, the UN *Declaration of Human Rights* seeks to protect the right to life of all. The descent into ever-greater destruction of human life is not the only possible future for us all. There is an alternative, which is based on respect for every person. This will entail both sacrifice and suffering, but I hope I have shown that it is the only path to a life worthy of human beings.

Contemporary developments in the biological sciences are fast-moving, so that both Churches and individuals constantly need to decide whether and how to make use of the new possibilities presented to them, especially in relation to human life. Experts, whether legislators, medical personnel or clergy can advise and inform, but in the end, the decision on whether to make use of these new developments normally rests with the ordinary person. That makes it important for every man and woman involved in these life-and-death decisions to inform themselves and consider the consequences of their actions, before making a decision.

I hope that this book will help anyone faced with one of these difficult choices to seek a solution that leads to a good life without sacrificing a human being in the process.

Notes

1   See A. Dowsing, *The Gift of Self in Marriage* (Leominster: Gracewing, 2007).

ACKNOWLEDGMENTS

MANY PEOPLE HAVE helped to shape this book through their prayers and comments, but I would like to thank the following in particular. Ruth Burrows (Sr Rachel of Quidenham) has accompanied me throughout my life as a writer, both by sharing her experience with me and praying for each project as it took shape. Judith Howman has commented on the book as I wrote it, thereby ensuring a much more readable text than I had originally sent her. In the course of our discussions, the fellow-members of my writers' group, Biddy Collyer, Gail Halley and Catherine Tye, have thrown light on many aspects of the book and helped me avoid several pitfalls.

I am also grateful to Rev. Dr Paul Haffner of Gracewing for steering me towards writing the book I was really meant to write. Above all, I want to thank my husband, Roy, for his unfailing support throughout the often difficult process of writing. Without his encouragement and practical help I would not have been able to complete this book. Finally, I am grateful for permission to reproduce the short poem from the article 'Blessings in abundance' by Sheila Hollins, published in *The Tablet* of 17/24 December 2005 (https://www.thetablet.co.uk).

NOTES

1. *Human life* means *innocent human life*.
2. *Ireland* refers to the *Irish Republic*.
3. Unless otherwise stated, Bible quotations are from: *The New Jerusalem Bible*, Standard Edition (London: Darton, Longman & Todd, 1985). Abbreviations of books of the Bible are mainly those used in *The New Jerusalem Bible*.
4. Quotations from the Psalms are from: *The Grail Psalms, A New Translation* (London: HarperCollins Publishers, 1991).
5. The quotations of Pope Emeritus Benedict are from: J. Ratzinger, *Co-Workers of the Truth* (San Francisco, Ignatius Press,1992), p. 50.
6. The quotation of Jeremiah is from: *A Shorter Prayer during the Day, The Psalter of the Divine Office*, (Glasgow, Collins, 1986), p. 66.

1 SEEKING A GOOD LIFE

GOOD LIFE IS what we all want, but what exactly is a good life and how do we find it? The last few years my husband and I have been going on holiday to a small hotel in the French Alps. It is run by an English couple who had decided to escape from the rat-race in the big city to live in the kind of surroundings that they liked and do what they really enjoyed. They cooked wonderful food for their guests, often eaten in the garden, with a view of the mountains as a backdrop. 'It's a good life', the wife said on one occasion. However, talking to them, it became quite clear that the move had not always been easy and that in the beginning they had had to sacrifice most of their free time to get their new venture off the ground. The good life had come at a price, it had been costly, but it had been worth the cost.

Life in the house in the French Alps is one model of a good life. It is real. It is true. It is possible to live life in this way. There is another model which we see again and again in television advertisements: the story line in such advertisements is always the same. Beautiful woman or handsome man glides through life effortlessly, because she or he has bought the product in question. If only you have the right make-up or the right car, the good life will be yours. The trouble with this model of life is that it is an illusion. It is a mirage. It is not true. We all know that life is hard and that a treatment or product will not buy us a good life, however much we sometimes wish it was so.

What Is a Good Life?

So what is a good life? If I asked somebody, 'How would you describe a good life?', that person might say, 'It's the kind of life I want'. That could mean all sorts of things, but for a lot of people it would mean the kind of work they wanted, enough money to live on comfortably and, above all, being happy in their relationships. However, there must surely be more than that to a good life, so I might ask them, 'What else would you want from a good life?' If the person I spoke to believed in the Ten Commandments, which say that you may not steal, that you may not commit adultery and that you may not kill, then living by those Commandments might well shape their idea of a good life. If they had lived by the Commandments, then they would have lived a good life, because they would have followed what they believed to be true. To put it more shortly, for them a good life would be a life lived in truth, which is how we define it in this book.

The Price of a Good Life

Ideally, everyone should have a good life, but in practice this can be difficult, because people do not live in little boxes. They influence each other. They do not achieve a good life in isolation. It is therefore necessary to seek a good life in such a way that it does not affect other people adversely. There are people who are willing to accept great hardship and suffering in order to respect the lives of every human being. They believe that this is the only way they themselves can lead a good life. On the other hand, there are those who decide to take human life, their own or that of others, in order to have a good life themselves. This applies particularly to the beginning and end of human life. For this second group, the destruction of human life becomes the price of a good life and increasing numbers belong in this group.

We therefore have two opposing bodies of opinion, one of which believes that everybody without exception has the right to life, while those belonging to the second group believe that some human beings have more of a right to life than others, or as George Orwell put it in *Animal Farm*, 'All animals are equal, but some animals are more equal than others'.[1] We will come back to the subject of an equal right to life many times in this book. (When we speak of human life, we always mean innocent human life).

What I Believe to be True

Decisions about the right to life depend on what each one of us believes is true. But is there one truth or many? If each individual has his or her own truth, then, in theory, there can be as many truths as there are individuals. Then truth becomes something entirely subjective and this is increasingly happening in our times. If, on the other hand, truth is something that exists independently of what each one of us believes, then there is something solid and unchangeable to hold on to. Then we have an objective truth to base our beliefs on and this kind of truth that the people who followed the Ten Commandments believed in. For Christians the teaching of Christ is objectively true. It is always true, regardless of what this or that person thinks about it.

Respect for the objective truth is crucial for achieving respect for all human life. If the right to life of everyone comes to depend on what each individual believes, then human life is at the mercy of many different personal opinions. This happens more and more often in the name of seeking a good life. If everyone's right to life is to be respected, then this right needs to be based on the objective truth about human life, a truth which is as solidly there as the ground I walk on; in fact, more solidly there, because no earthquake can change it.

The Christian Model for a Good Life

The Bible gives us two accounts of how God created man and woman and of the good life that he intended for them, from the very beginning. The first account describes in poetic form how God created an ordered world in which each individual part was in harmony with all the other parts. The whole of this description could be called God's blueprint or model for a good life.[2]

After separating light from darkness, God creates the sea and the dry land and then all the plants and the animals that live on the Earth. Finally the account moves on to the creation of man himself, the crowning glory of all that God has made. In this description, we see a progression from inanimate objects, to plant life, to animals, to mankind and each step is followed by the refrain, 'God saw that it was good.'

However, man and woman are creatures of a completely different order to all the rest. This is what the Bible says,

> God said, 'Let us make man in our own image, in
> the likeness of ourselves, and let them be masters
> of [all the animals]'.[3]
> God created man in the image of himself,
> In the image of God he created him,
> Male and female he created them.[4]

This new creature is fundamentally different from all the others, because man and woman are created in the 'image and likeness' of God himself.[5] This whole account is a reflection on the order and goodness of Creation and is not intended as a literal description of how the world was made.[6] What it does mean is that, from the beginning, life was meant to be good for all of Creation and especially for man and woman who are God-like creatures. Nevertheless, they are created beings who have received life and all their abilities from God. They are called to live in loving co-operation with God. They are called to live in truth. But precisely because they are God-like creatures, they can also choose to reject the truth. They can choose to live a lie. This comes out particularly clearly in the second account of Creation.

In the second account, we see man and woman, Adam and Eve, in the Garden of Eden, where everything they need is provided for them. The one thing they may not do is to eat the fruit of the 'tree of the knowledge of good and evil'.[7] This is because, by eating this fruit, they will attempt to put themselves in God's place. They will therefore reject their status as created beings and and try to live as if they had created themselves. As we all know, Adam and Eve do eat the fruit (the Fall) and must take the consequences. These are not, as they had hoped, that they are now in control of their lives, but rather that life becomes cumbersome and full of conflicts between people. Human beings begin to destroy life in order to have what they think of as a good life.

The Bible illustrates this with the story of the two brothers Cain and Abel, the sons of Adam and Eve. Cain believes that God prefers Abel, so that he envies his brother and eventually kills him.[8] The important message here is that Cain gets rid of another person, who seems to get in his way. This pattern has repeated itself in many different forms down the ages and it is the root of the threats to human life that form the main topic of this book.

After the Fall, the Creator did not give up on his damaged Creation. Put very simply, the whole of the rest of the Scriptures describes how God patiently began to heal the consequences of the Fall, so that mankind could return to a life in harmony with its Creator and with each other, that is, a good life. The culmination of this healing process was the birth of Christ, the Son of God, as a human being. Christ was to live an ordinary human life in total obedience to the will of God, so that he would become a model or example for everyone to follow. However, he taught not only through the way he lived, but also through his teaching, which often took the form of stories.

The Good Samaritan

In the well-known story of the Good Samaritan Jesus gives us a model of what it means to lead a good life.

A lawyer comes to Jesus, asking how to lead a life worthy of eternal life, that is, a good life.[9] In reply, Jesus prompts him to quote what the Jews knew as the greatest commandment of the Law,

> You must love the Lord your God with all your heart, with all your soul, with all your strength, and with all your mind, and your neighbour as yourself.[10]

'Do this and life is yours', Jesus says, but then the man asks, 'Who is my neighbour?[11]

(We can almost hear the lawyer thinking, 'Is it anybody at all, or just my family and friends – my sort of people?'). Jesus then tells the story of the Good Samaritan, a story that has become a model for all neighbourly love:

> A man was walking from Jerusalem to Jericho, when he was attacked by robbers and left for dead by the side of the road. Two Temple officials saw the man, but ignored him. Then a Samaritan came across the man, and, moved with compassion, he bandaged the man's wounds, put him on his own mount, and took him to an inn, where he paid the

innkeeper to look after him. Leaving money for the
man's keep, he promised to refund any additional
expenses on his return.

At the end of the story, Jesus asks the lawyer which of the
three men had been a neighbour to the wounded man.
The lawyer replies, 'The one who showed pity towards
him'.[12] 'Do the same yourself', Jesus tells him.[13]

According to the story of the Samaritan, the test of a
good life, the kind of life that merits eternal life, is, above
all, love of one's neighbour; and the neighbour can be
absolutely anybody. It is significant that the man who is
attacked on the road is described simply as 'a man',
without any further distinction. He is Everyman; and the
Samaritan goes to great trouble to help him. A good life
will therefore frequently be a life that involves inconvenience, or even pain and suffering, as we shall see in future
chapters. For the moment, it is enough to say that, in our
times in particular, our neighbour will often be the
embryo, the unborn child, and the handicapped or sick
person. These are all as helpless as the man left unconscious on the road to Jericho, and all call for compassionate action on our part.

The Samaritan helps to save the wounded man's life
and respect for a person's life is the most fundamental
aspect of neighbourly love. It is therefore not surprising
that the Catholic Church has spoken up strongly for the
right to life of every human being from conception to
natural death. However, the Church is not alone in seeking
to uphold the right to life. The United Nations (UN), too,
has done much to protect human life, especially by trying
to defend human rights throughout the world. These
rights are expressed in what is known as the Universal
Declaration of Human Rights.

The Universal Declaration of Human Rights

Conditions during the Second World War had shown only too clearly what life was like when it was not good. Already during the War, the US president Franklin D. Roosevelt, had taken steps towards establishing a United Nations, a name which he coined. He did not live to see this organisation come into being, but, soon after the War, in October 1945, representatives of fifty nations met in San Francisco to found the United Nations (UN). In 1946 Roosevelt's widow, Eleanor Roosevelt, was appointed as the only woman delegate to this new body. Mrs Roosevelt had been a lifelong human rights campaigner, so that it was fitting that she should be given the task of chairing the United Nations Human Rights Commission, which drew up the Universal Declaration of Human Rights. Its adoption by the UN General Assembly in December 1948 was a historic moment, as the Declaration was the first of its kind in the world.[14]

The Declaration stressed that all human beings have been given reason and conscience and that they should therefore act towards each other 'in a spirit of brother-hood' or, in Christian terms, 'with neighbourly love.'[15]

The universal rights included access to food, shelter, education and also freedom of belief and opinion. These rights belonged to everyone, simply because they were human. Above all, the Declaration claimed the right to life for all, a right without which none of the other rights have any meaning.[16] The Declaration also outlined the human duties which keep the exercise of rights in balance, so that one person's rights will not be bought at the expense of another person's life or health.[17] The fact that the Declaration was accepted without anyone voting against reveals the level of approval for the principles it contains.

In theory at least, everyone's human rights should be respected. However, a number of terms used in the

Declaration, above all the word 'everyone' itself, are not clearly defined, which has lead to difficulties with the application of human rights. As we shall see, this is true especially with regard to the rights of human beings before birth. For instance, if a foetus has severe abnormalities, what, then, are his or her rights, as against the rights of others to perform an abortion?

Secular and Religious Concepts of a Good Life

While much of the Declaration of Human Rights is in fundamental agreement with Christian principles, both the Bible and Church documents go beyond a purely natural foundation for the rights and duties expressed in the Declaration. Being created in the image of God implies a right to live as a 'God-like' creature, but also a duty to live in a way that is worthy of such a creature.

Many non-Christian religions follow principles of human rights and duties similar to those of Christianity. For instance, Hindu belief places a strong emphasis on the performance of duties, above all duties to society. Gandhi made the following comment in connection with the Declaration,

> I learnt from my illiterate but wise mother that all rights … came from duty well done. Thus, the very right to life accrues to us only when we do the duty of citizenship in the world.[18]

Islam, too, has teachings about human rights. In the *Universal Islamic Declaration of Human Rights*, Muslim experts have formulated human rights on a basis of the Qur'an and examples of the life of the Prophet Muhammad. With regard to the right to life they have stated that,

> Human life is sacred and inviolable and every effort shall be made to protect it. In particular no one

shall be exposed to injury or death, except under
the authority of the Law.[19]

We can now see that there is considerable agreement
about the right to life and the duty to protect innocent
human life, both from secular and religious perspectives.
However, in our times, there is a widespread tendency to
claim human rights at the cost of human duties. This
over-emphasis on rights, often combined with a disregard
for an objective truth, can become the basis for a purely
personal system of values, that is, a subjective ethics.

A Subjective Ethics: My Private Beliefs

A subjective ethics is not one system, but many. Indeed,
it can hardly be called a system at all, as, in theory, there
could be as many systems of subjective ethics as there are
people. For someone who follows a subjective ethics, a
good life is often a life based on choices that appear to be
right for a particular person in a particular set of circumstances. There can therefore be no generally accepted
norm for right and wrong, only what seems right for this
individual; and this is particularly true in the areas of
reproduction and end-of-life issues, where the right to
choose has become a watchword.

When people believe in a subjective ethics, they tend
to see a good life as a life without any obstacle to what they
want to do. They aim to be in total control. Much advertising today makes the assumption that people do not want
to put up with any inconvenience. It presents a model of
life that it believes many people aspire to.

This model can become a threat to life when the good
life that one person wants can only be achieved at the price
of someone else's life. This is the case when a handicapped
or unwanted foetus is aborted, because he or she is per-

ceived as a threat to the good life of the mother or parents. The same applies to the growing number of sick or disabled people who now campaign for the right to be helped to die. In these latter cases the threat is, of course, to a person's own life rather than that of someone else. A different type of threat exists where terrorists believe that they have the right to kill others in order to achieve a particular goal.

The loss of a shared faith based on the objective truth has had serious consequences for many vulnerable human beings. This matters to all of us, because at some stage we will all become vulnerable. We are all going to become like the man left for dead by the side of the road from Jerusalem to Jericho. Whether we live or die will then depend on whether others consider our lives worth saving and on whether they believe we are worth the cost.

Conclusion

Until fairly recently there was considerable agreement between the teaching of Christianity (and many other religions) and the beliefs of individuals about human rights and duties. In particular, there was a general assumption that human life should not be taken in order to further the rights of another person. This assumption was expressed in law, so that, for instance, abortion and euthanasia were illegal.

In our times, more and more people assume that individuals have the right to live according to their own understanding of right and wrong, rather than following an objective, shared belief. Truth has become a matter for the individual. As we shall see in future chapters, this development has, in its turn, influenced legislation, so that the law in the West often diverges from the teaching of Christianity. It is also beginning to part company with some of the principles of the Declaration of Human Rights.

Public opinion rather than religious belief and adherence to an objective truth has come to drive changes in legislation. Once an opinion has become enshrined in law, it is often perceived as expressing what is morally right. ('It's legal, so it must be all right!'). The law further influences popular opinion, which in its turn influences the law, so that there is a circular development, gaining an ever stronger momentum. In this context the individual has an unprecedented responsibility, because the combined views of many individuals have the power to drive social developments in new directions, both for good and for ill.

Overall Summary

- There are many possible definitions of a good life, but in this book we have defined it as a life lived in truth. Christ's life is the supreme example of such a life.
- The story of the Samaritan shows that, in order to live a good life, it is necessary to accept inconvenience and even suffering.
- The *Declaration of Human Rights* reflects much of Christian belief, above all the right to life of everyone.
- Many in today's subjectively oriented society believe that human life cannot be good, if it does not correspond to a desired model of a healthy and handicap-free life.
- There is a growing conviction that it can be morally defensible to take human life for the sake of a good life. This stands in opposition to the Christian teaching that a good life for all is only possible when the right to life of everyone is respected.

In the following chapters we will turn to the question of how these developments have come to threaten human life, and what individuals and religious groups can do to counteract the threats, thereby protecting human life.

Notes

1. G. Orwell, *Animal Farm* (London: Penguin Books, 1951), Chapter 10.
2. Gn. 1:1–2:4a.
3. Gn 1:26. The plural form used to refer to God may express 'the majesty and fullness of God's being; the common name for God in Hebrew is elohim, a plural form. See note k to this verse in *The New Jerusalem Bible* (London: Darton, Longman & Todd, 1985).
4. Gn 1:27.
5. Gn 1:26.
6. *The New Jerusalem Bible*, note (a) to Chapter One of Genesis.
7. Gn 2:17.
8. Gn 4:1-8.
9. Lk 10:25.
10. Lk 10:27.
11. Lk 10:29.
12. Lk 10:37.
13. Lk 10:37.
14. D. P. Forsythe, *Human Rights in International Relations* (Cambridge: Cambridge University Press, 2000), p. 36.
15. Universal Declaration of Human Rights Article 1. http://www.un.org/Overview/rights.html. (28 September 2005).
16. Universal Declaration of Human Rights Articles 3, http://www.un.org/Overview/rights.html. (28 September 2005).
17. Universal Declaration of Human Rights Article 29, http://www.un.org/Overview/rights.html. (28 September 2005).
18. G. Arciniegas, 'CultureA Human Right', in Freedom and Culture, ed. J. Huxley, (London: A. Wingate, 1951), p. 32.
19. 'Universal Islamic Declaration of Human Rights', Paris 1981, I 'Right to Life', section (a) on http://www.alhewar.com/ ISLAMDECL.html (9 July 2010).

PART I

THREATS TO HUMAN LIFE

INTRODUCTION TO PART I

W HEN HUMAN LIFE is under threat, it has always been a great joy to save it. After the terror attacks in Paris in 2015, in which 130 people were killed and well over 300 injured, everyone pulled together to save as many lives at possible. People queued up at the hospitals to give blood and, as the wounded were brought in, doctors from all over Paris rushed to offer their assistance too. Their one thought was to save the lives that could be saved.

We all have a natural instinct to preserve life, rather than to destroy it. It is not for nothing that murder is considered the worst of all crimes. And yet, there are some human beings that are increasingly thought to be not worth keeping alive. The embryo and unborn child belong to this group, as do many of the disabled and sick. The instinct to save life that was so much in evidence after the Paris attacks does not always make itself felt when it comes to humans at the beginning and end of life. In our times many people believe that they have the right to destroy such lives in order to have a good life. The question is then no longer, 'Can we save this life?' but, 'Is this life worth saving?' For terrorists, anyone who gets in the way of their goals loses his or her right to life.

Part I of this book describes the new threats to human life that are the result of assuming a right to destroy some of the most vulnerable human lives, for the sake of having a good life. In order to understand some of the thinking that drives contemporary threats to human life, this part concludes with a chapter on eugenic killings in the past, especially in Nazi Germany. It is particularly disturbing that (with the exception of terrorism) the destructions of human life for the sake of a good life are either legal or in the process of becoming so. It is precisely their legality that makes them such a threat to human life, because once a practise is legal, many people will think it is acceptable.

These threats to human life are certainly disturbing, but are they really new? To some extent there has always been a threat to human life for the sake of a perceived good life. For instance, abortion has been carried out since ancient times in order to avoid scandal or because another child was seen as a burden. Euthanasia has taken place out of (misguided) compassion for someone who is suffering. It is also reasonable to assume that terrorism has always existed in some form. However, there are some important differences between the threats that exist in our times and those that existed formerly, even within living memory.

Firstly, the creation of embryos outside the womb, in vitro (IVF), is a relatively new technique, so that the threat to the lives of embryos that are not implanted is also new. Secondly, the widespread legalisation of abortion and, in some countries, assisted suicide and euthanasia, is a comparatively new phenomenon. Thirdly, the spread of terrorism on an international scale is new. In all these cases, individual men and women have a growing power over life and death, because they are the ones who decide whether or not to make use of IVF with its associated embryo destruction, of abortion and of assisted suicide and euthanasia. They are also the ones who decide whether or not to support or engage in terrorism.

The contemporary threat to human life, especially from embryo destruction and abortion, is huge. Let us take just one example: During the first ten years of the twenty-first century there were approximately 200,000 abortions each year in the UK alone. By comparison, the total estimated deaths from the bombings of Hiroshima and Nagasaki were 100,000, that is, only half the number of recent UK abortions.[1] However, the decisions to bomb the two Japanese cities were taken at government level, whereas the decisions to use the biomedical procedures that destroy human life rests largely with private individuals. That is why it is important to draw attention to the widespread threats to life for the sake of a good life that are, with the exception of terrorism, too often gaining acceptance as part of normal life today. This acceptance stands in direct opposition to our natural instinct to preserve life and to the joy that most of us feel when someone in danger is saved.

In the chapters that follow we will describe the threats to the child in the womb and to the lives of the handicapped and sick, comparing the latter with the killing of the sick and handicapped in Nazi Germany that so shocked the world; but first we will turn to the human life whose destruction often goes unnoticed, that is, the embryo.

Notes

[1] 'The Atomic Bombings of Hiroshima and Nagasaki', http://www.atomicarchive.com/Docs/MED/med_chp10.shtml (21 March 2011). Department of Health, Abortion Statistics England and Wales: 2006, http://www.dh.gov.uk/en/ Publication-sandstatistics/ Publications/ PublicationsStatistics/DH_075697 (21 March 2011). See Pope Francis, *Discourse at Hiroshima* (24 November 2019): 'Here, in an incandescent burst of lightning and fire, so many men and women, so many dreams and hopes, disappeared, leaving behind only shadows and silence. In barely an instant, everything was devoured by a black hole of destruction and death. From that abyss of silence, we continue even today to hear the cries of those who are no longer.'

2 THREATS TO HUMAN LIFE: THE EMBRYO

'**D**O YOU WANT to know what Jesus looked like?' With this opening remark to his talk the eminent consultant had certainly got our attention. I can still remember the silence in the audience as we waited for his revelation. 'Did this man have inside information?', we wondered.

Then he showed us a picture of the early embryo. 'This is what Jesus looked like just after he was conceived', he said. We could not have been told more clearly that there was no stage of human development that Jesus had not shared and that he was fully there, as a person, right from his conception. He was a very young person, of course, but the picture of the embryo was most certainly a picture of what Jesus had looked like at that stage of his life.

This is how we all begin. We are totally there, as unique persons, from the moment of conception. That was how this specialist saw the embryo, it is what many Christians believe and it is what the Catholic Church teaches about the origin of every human being. As we shall see, this understanding of the beginning of human life is also borne out by research into the development of the human embryo.

However, many people believe that the embryo is not yet a human being. Until recently their view had not affected life in the real world. After all, the embryo only existed inside a woman's body, where it could not normally be observed. The question of who or what the embryo was had remained largely theoretical. This changed with the development of the *in vitro* method of fertilisation (IVF). Now embryos could be created in the laboratory, which opened a whole Pandora's box of new threats to human life. (Pandora was the mythical lady who opened a box she was not supposed to open, thereby letting out all manner of human ills.)

Nevertheless, the motivation for developing this new method of conception could not have been more idealistic. It was intended to help childless couples have a child. It was because some women could not conceive naturally that the two British doctors, Robert Edwards and Patrick Steptoe, began to investigate the possibility of creating an embryo outside a woman's body and then transferring it into her womb. In 1978 they achieved their first successful pregnancy. Louise Brown, the world's first test-tube baby, had been born. This was seen as a triumph for medical science and it was indeed a joy for the many couples who would now be able to have the child they thought they would never have. What could possibly be wrong with such a wonderful new treatment?

Sadly, there is a downside to this new method of conception. It always involves creating more embryos than are implanted. Sometimes these spare embryos are frozen for later use, but many end up being destroyed. The question about the status of the embryo therefore now has a very practical application. If the embryo is only a potential human being, then the IVF method might be acceptable. On the other hand, if the embryo is a human being, then embryo destruction is unacceptable. Thus decisions about the creation and treatment of embryos depend on whether they are considered fully human or not.

In Vitro Fertilisation

Let us look at the IVF method in a little more detail. Typically, it involves harvesting about ten eggs from the woman's body, which are then fertilised in glass dishes, hence the term *in vitro* meaning *in glass*. After some forty-eight hours the most promising embryos are re-implanted in the mother's womb. Here we see the beginning of the quality control of human embryos that reveals one of the fundamental problems with the IVF method.

The quality control is taken a step further with the introduction of Pre-implantation Genetic Diagnosis (PGD). This technique has been developed to help eradicate some of the most serious inherited diseases. As with basic IVF, several embryos are created, but only those that are not carriers of a particular disease or disorder are implanted, while the rest are destroyed. Again, the intention with the procedure is good. The parents and medical personnel want to spare a child from the suffering of living with serious disease, but in the process they destroy the handicapped embryos that have been created.

If the development of PGD has sinister implications, then this is even more true of another recent use of IVF. In some countries human embryos are now created solely for research purposes, so that in these cases any link between the IVF method and a live birth is broken.

All these threats to embryonic human life have come about through what might be called the 'Pandora's box effect.' For every new development of the IVF technique, however well-intentioned, a new threat has appeared. Whether or not such a threat can be justified, depends on whether the embryo is considered a human being with the same rights as other humans or whether it is regarded only as a cluster of cells that may become a human being in the future. At the heart of the debate about IVF is the clash between advances in medical science on the one hand and the rights of the embryo on the other.

When does Human Life Begin?

In order to decide how to treat the embryo, we need to understand when human life begins. The dictionary definition of a human being is 'a member of any of the races of *Homo Sapiens*,' but this definition does not tell us anything about when a human being comes into existence. Is it at conception, at birth, or at some point in-between? Both scientists and theologians have considered this question and we will begin by looking at it from the point of view of the scientist. When does the embryo begin to exist?

A study of how the embryo develops from conception onwards can tell us a great deal about its nature and, above all, about whether the embryo can be regarded as a human being. Everyone knows, in very general terms, that the embryo begins with the fusion of sperm and egg; but what actually takes place at this point? The embryologist Maureen Condic has described this event in a recent article, beginning with an account of what happens at the fusion of sperm and egg.[1] At this point a new cell is formed which behaves differently to both sperm and egg cells. It is not just a new type of cell, but it is a cell which behaves like a living organism.[2] Granted, it is a very immature organism. It neither looks like, nor behaves like a mature human being, but it carries within itself the blueprint for a mature human body. No other cells have this property. For instance, if we grow a skin cell in a culture, it will only ever produce more skin cells.

Because of the unique properties of the embryo, there is a continuum of development of the same living organism, from the fusion of sperm and egg, to the birth of a child and on through adulthood to death.[3] This means that, biologically speaking, placing the beginning of human life at any point other than conception is an arbitrary decision. On a basis of the biological evidence, the beginning of human life must necessarily be placed at the fusion of sperm and egg, at conception. Therefore the one-cell embryo that comes into existence at that point is a living member of the human race, a human being.

As we shall see, not everyone agrees with this definition of the embryo and we will return to this topic later, but first let us consider the fate of this young human being in today's world.

IVF Treatment and the Fate of Spare Embryos

As we have seen, the embryo is not always treated with the respect due to a human being, as he or she is routinely destroyed in connection with IVF. In order to illustrate the scale of the problem of embryo destruction associated with this procedure, let us compare embryo deaths linked to IVF treatment in the UK and US with the incidence of road deaths in the same two countries over a period of some fifteen years.

Between 1991 and 2005, the embryo wastage in the UK was well over a million.[4] Over the same period, there were 50,000 road deaths in the UK. This means that there were over twenty times more human embryo deaths during the period than there were road deaths.[5]

We do not have precise figures for the number of embryos left over from IVF treatment in the US, but, on a basis of available information, there were at least some seven million embryo deaths in that country between 1996 and 2006.[6] If these deaths are compared with the approximately half a million traffic fatalities in the US over the same period, there were fourteen times as many embryo deaths in the US as traffic deaths.[7] Thus the wastage of embryos is huge both in the UK and the US.

The enormous wastage of human embryos associated with IVF is not the central problem, because, if the one-cell embryo is a human being, then even the destruction of one embryo is unjustifiable. In order to accept the procedure, it is necessary to believe either that it is permissible to kill a human being or that the embryo is not yet a human being. Therefore the central question in relation to IVF is not about the efficiency of the method, but about the status of the embryo.

A doctor working with IVF has put the problem succinctly. In an interview about her work she said,

> Life should be respected differently at different stages. A fertilised egg is not a life; it is a potential life. I can't prove this, but my work is based on it. If I felt that every fertilised egg that I created for IVF was an individual person, I couldn't do my job. We create hundreds of embryos every week; eight to ten for each person, only ever using two.[8]

She has pointed to the crux of the matter: If the embryo is a human being, albeit a very immature one, then killing an embryo is killing a human being. Therefore this doctor is only prepared to do her job, because she does not believe the embryo is a human being. However, as we have seen, the continuous development of the human embryo from the one-cell stage onwards has demonstrated that a human being does indeed exist from the very moment of conception.

Some scientists have sought to justify the embryo destruction associated with IVF by pointing out that there is also considerable embryo wastage with natural conception.[9] However, there is a fundamental difference between the two cases, because embryo deaths with natural conception are accidental, whereas embryo deaths using IVF are the consequence of the deliberate creation of embryos that may never be implanted.

Genetic Screening and IVF

A certain amount of screening always takes place in connection with IVF. The selection process becomes genetic screening when it is carried out in order to avoid transmitting an inherited disease, so that only non-carriers of the disease are implanted. In recent years the UK Human Fertilisation and Embryology Authority (HFEA) has allowed genetic screening of embryos in order to eliminate some serious inherited conditions. This is selective breeding or eugenics by stealth.

In May 2006 *The Times'* front page carried the banner headline: 'First Baby in Britain Designed Cancer-free'. The article was about the genetic screening of embryos that were potential carriers of an inherited form of eye cancer. The readers were told that a woman who was a carrier of the cancer was now expecting a healthy child as a result of genetic screening.[10]

The article hailed the screening as a great step forward, but also pointed to its controversial nature, as it would lead to the destruction of some embryos that would never develop the disease, 'if they were allowed to develop into children.'[11] The implication is that embryos are at least potential children.

In November of the same year, the paper reported the delivery of healthy twins to a couple who were both carriers of cystic fibrosis. Again, the embryos were conceived outside the womb and screened before being implanted. The clinical director of the PGD programme,

Professor Peter Braude, was quoted as saying that the use of PGD meant the best chance of avoiding 'the need for termination of the pregnancy', if the foetus was found to have a serious genetic disorder.[12]

It is significant, if he has been quoted correctly, that the Professor used the term 'need' about the termination, as if it could be taken for granted that a child carrying a serious genetic disorder would have to be aborted. Maybe it was a slip of the tongue, but it would appear that, with such a comment, we are on the threshold of an attitude that takes it for granted that some babies have to be aborted, in other words, eugenics.

The use of PGD also raises the question of the value of the handicapped or seriously ill person. Once the destruction of a sick embryo has been legalised, it becomes easier to legalise the killing of very sick human beings after birth, as is already happening with some newborns and in the later stages of life too.

Embryos for Experimentation

The embryo is an ideal medium for medical or biological research, because components of it can grow into any kind of cell, for instance a skin cell, which can then be used in the treatment of disease. When the embryo has served its purpose, it is destroyed, so that this form of research always leads to the death of the embryo. The UK has the questionable honour of being the only country in Europe where it is legal, with the consent of the parents, to create embryos that will only ever be used for research. With this development the lack of respect for the human embryo has surely reached its lowest point.

The Embryo and the Law: UK, US and Ireland

The right to life is one of the fundamental human rights, but for the embryo, the most vulnerable of all human beings, this right is rarely respected. There are regulations which protect the embryo to some extent, but these are mainly about how others should treat the embryo rather than rights that belong to the embryo itself. However, as we shall see later, the embryo is occasionally granted some protection of its own.

In 1990 the UK became the first country in the world to introduce regulation for fertility treatment and therefore also for how the embryo should be treated. The new regulating authority, the HFEA, had the powers to licence the creation of embryos and also to freeze embryos for later use.[13] These powers were meant to help childless couples have a child. They were intended to create life. However, the HFEA was later given the power to licence the creation of embryos solely for research purposes, so that the authority had deviated from its original purpose of helping to create life. In 2008 this nightmare scenario went even further, when Parliament legalised the creation of embryos based on a combination of human and animal material. Again, these embryos were intended solely for research. *Brave New World* had arrived in the UK.[14]

In the US, the fate of the embryo depends partly on federal and partly on state legislation. (Federal legislation applies to the whole of the US, while state legislation applies only to individual states.) Experimentation on embryos is legal in the whole of the US, but severely restricted in practice, because federal funds may not be used for research leading to embryo destruction.[15] This means that, even when individual states permit embryo experimentation, this is often prevented by lack of funding. The tension between federal and state governments about the treatment of the embryo reflects a tension within the population about the morality of experimenting on the human embryo and we will return to this topic later.

Unlike many other countries, Ireland once had a constitution which guaranteed the right to life of the unborn child. We might therefore expect the embryo to be better protected in that country than anywhere else. However, legal protection depends on how the embryo is defined in law. This became clear after a court case between an estranged husband and wife about the fate of the couple's three embryos, stored in a fertility clinic. After the estrangement, the wife still wanted to have the embryos implanted, whereas the husband refused to give his consent. She therefore took him to court, basing her case on the fact that the Irish Constitution protected the right to life of the unborn child. However, the judge ruled that the Constitution did not provide for the protection of embryos created via IVF. Thus, even in a country that protects the right to life of the unborn child, the life of the human embryo conceived via IVF is not protected.[16]

These examples show that, once embryos have been created outside the mother's body, they cannot depend on the law to protect their right to life. Indeed, as we have seen, the law has now begun to sanction the creation of embryos who will be killed, once they have served their purpose. In relation to the embryo, much legislation has come to reflect the saying that the end justifies the means. This is not everyone's opinion, but it does appear to be the opinion of the majority.

One way of gauging the beliefs of a population is through opinion polls. These are not always reliable, but they do constitute a significant indicator of the beliefs of ordinary people. It will therefore be helpful to look at some information about attitudes to the embryo from British and American polls.

Public Opinion and the Embryo: UK and US

IVF

The only UK opinion poll about IVF available at the time of writing is a survey of 1000 readers carried out by a women's magazine in 2011. This small poll is, however, highly revealing of women's attitudes. As public funding for IVF varies from one local authority to another, two thirds of the respondents said that they would move house in order to gain access to the procedure; the implication is that they approved of it and would use it if they felt they needed it. The editor of the magazine stated that every time they ran a story about infertility and IVF, they were inundated with letters from readers desperate to use the procedure, but unable to do so because of where they lived.[17]

A recent experience brought this home to me. I was on a plane returning from abroad, when I got talking to the woman sitting next to me. The conversation turned to IVF and she mentioned her daughter's difficulties in conceiving. 'But then', she said, 'after the third attempt, she got pregnant and now has a lovely baby girl.' I did not have the heart to mention the embryos that would have been lost. It seemed neither the time nor the place.

However, I believe her comments were typical of what many people, probably most, think of IVF. They see it as a treatment for infertility without realising that it involves the destruction of many embryos that are not implanted. If they were aware of the full implications of IVF, they might hesitate to use the procedure, however hard such a decision would be.

PGD

As we have seen, there is at least some approval in the UK for the PGD technique, which involves discarding disease-carrying embryos in favour of healthy ones. This has also been my impression from speaking to people with a serious inherited disease in the family. They have told me again and again that they do not want any child of theirs to be burdened with the faulty gene. This is very understandable, but the problem is whether it is right to avoid a child growing up with a serious illness or handicap at the cost of the lives of affected embryonic children.

Unlike the UK, the US has no government regulation of PGD, so that each IVF provider decides, together with the patient, whether testing for specific conditions is appropriate. A survey of clinics in 2006 found that most of these use PGD for a range of disorders. The reasons why some clinics did not provide PGD are interesting. The survey showed that practical considerations, such as inadequate resources and lack of demand, vastly overshadowed moral or ethical reasons. Therefore it seems that those in charge clinics considered the PGD procedure to be value neutral.

Two years earlier, in 2004, there had been a survey of the opinions of some 5,000 typical Americans about the use of PGD in various circumstances. About two thirds approved of the procedure to avoid a fatal disease or to find a *saviour sibling*, that is, a tissue donor, for a sick brother or sister. Less than half approved of PGD for sex selection, whereas less than a third approved of a hypothetical test for intelligence or strength.[18] Thus the desire to avoid a fatal disease or to heal a sick brother or sister was the strongest motivation for approval of PGD. Selection on a basis of sex or intelligence was far less acceptable, probably because this was seen to be a step too far towards a *Brave New World.*

The Views of Handicapped People

The use of PGD is based on the assumption that people with handicaps or serious diseases would rather not have been born. However, this is far from always the case. An article based on a 2014 survey in the US has pointed out that many who had developed the diseases for which PGD can test felt that their lives were well worth living, despite their handicap or disease. As in the UK, people in these groups feared that those with disabilities would come to be considered second-class citizens and a burden to society. For this reason some groups rejected the technique completely, because it could so easily be misused as a means of genetic screening.[19]

I once read a description of an imaginary scene where a mother was out with a handicapped child in a pushchair. Another woman comes past, looks at the child and thinks, 'How could she?' The other woman meant, of course, 'How could she let this child be born?' This is the kind of attitude that many handicapped people fear.

The Responsibility of Ordinary People

It is not only polls that reveal public opinion. In 2004 there was a series of lively debates about PGD in town halls across America called 'The Ethical Town Hall'. Large numbers of Americans from all walks of life, including health professionals, took part, which shows how much interest there is in this subject.

The issues surrounding genetic testing are complex and often difficult for lay people to understand. Yet it is precisely the non-specialists, who have to decide whether to use such testing and how to act on the results of the tests. In order to make an informed decision, participants also said that they needed first-hand accounts of the experiences of those who were living with the disorder they might want to test for.[20]

Those who came to the meeting made it clear that not only did they not know enough themselves, but, worse still, that the experts they expected to be able to advise them often did not fully understand what was involved either. They therefore called for better information for themselves as well as for those who advised them, such as doctors, clergy and counsellors.'

The discussions did not deal with the question of whether genetic testing should take place at all. Nevertheless, the demand by these ordinary Americans to be given the means of making responsible decisions about the use of PGD suggests that they might also be willing to consider the morality of making these tests at all. We will return to the topic of the life and death decisions that ordinary people face today in connection with the later stages of life too.

Religious Belief and the Status of the Embryo

When we plant a seed in the garden or in a pot, we expect it to grow into a flower or tree. We expect the seed to have the blueprint for the fully grown plant or tree and something similar applies to the development of the embryo.

From a scientific point of view, the most important fact about the human embryo is that, from the moment of conception, it carries a blueprint for continuous development from life in the mother's womb, to birth, to childhood and adulthood. The embryo is therefore a human being. It is a young human being, but as fully human as the adult he or she will one day become. The biological structure of the embryo is radically different from the sperm and egg cells from which it has been created, because these could not develop into a foetus on their own. From the point of view of biology alone, there are therefore compelling reasons to respect an embryo as much as an older human being.

This was also what the biblical authors believed about the development of the human being. They obviously did not know exactly how this development took place. The picture of the early embryo that we outlined would not have meant anything to them; but the idea that a particular person began in his mother's womb was perfectly understood. The Bible is full of stories about people who were called to a specific task right from the moment of conception. This is true above all of Jesus, but also of many of the prophets who had gone before him.

In what follows we will concentrate on Christian beliefs, but we will also give an outline of what some non-Christians believe about the embryo.

Evidence from the Bible

In Biblical times there was a firm belief that every human person had a specific vocation from the moment of conception. The account of the calling of the prophet Jeremiah in the Old Testament provides a particularly striking illustration of this,

> The word of Yahweh [God] came to me, saying:
> 'Before I formed you in the womb I knew you;
> before you came to birth I consecrated you,
> I appointed you as a prophet to the nations.'[21]

This passage clearly reveals Jeremiah's conviction that God had a plan for him, before he even created him; in other words, God was at work in the prophet as soon as he was conceived. Jeremiah cannot have understood, biologically, what happened at that point, but nevertheless he believed that his identity and vocation began when he was created. The belief in the existence of the human person from conception can also be seen in the account of the Annunciation in the New Testament. The angel, God's messenger, comes to Mary to invite her to become the mother of Jesus, saying,

> You are to conceive in your womb and bear a son, and you must name him Jesus. He ... will be called Son of the Most High.[22]

'Let your will be done', Mary says and she conceives. The child she now carries is Jesus in embryonic form; but he is the same person, who will one day reveal himself as the Son of God.

Catholic Teaching

The Catholic Church has always followed the biblical belief in the existence of the human person from conception onwards.[23] Because of the new developments in human fertilisation and embryology, the Church has restated its teaching in new documents. For instance, in 1987 the Church published a document, entitled *The Gift of Life* (*Donum Vitae*), which made it clear that a human being could not be made human somewhere down the line of its development. It was either human from the beginning or it was not human at all.[24]

It is significant that the authors of the document link the teaching of the Church with the findings of modern science which have demonstrated that fertilisation creates a new human individual. In this document science and theology come together as complementary methods of understanding the human person, each supporting the other's truth.[25] On the basis of this truth, it follows that it is never right to destroy an embryo, whether in connection with IVF or PGD or for research or for any other purpose, since all human beings have the right to life.

What does the Church say about the many children who have been born as a result of IVF? In their document *Cherishing Life*, the Bishops of England and Wales have made it abundantly clear that the Church does not in any way blame the children for the manner of their conception. At the same time they call for more research into the root causes of infertility, in order to remove the use of IVF.

The bishops also point to the danger of using PGD, because what begins as a well-intentioned attempt to remove serious inherited disease can easily become a policy of selecting only perfect human beings for survival.[26] With regard to the creation of human embryos for research purposes only, the document describes this as 'a crime against human beings.'[27] Not many people would condone this crime, if the embryos concerned were further advanced in their development and therefore looked more obviously human.

Non-Catholic Christian Perspectives

According to an official report, most Anglicans would find IVF acceptable, if it did not involve embryo destruction.[28] Others, however, believe that the soul does not enter the unborn child till some time later in his or her development, so that they are able to justify embryo destruction and also, as we shall see, abortion in some cases.[29] Anglican acceptance of IVF therefore depends on when human life is thought to begin and even in official documents there is no unified stance on this.

It is fitting to end this section with the moving words of a contemporary embryologist and Evangelical Christian, Professor John Wyatt. This is how he has described his own path to the conviction that the human person, body and soul, begins with conception. His comments refer both to the foetus and the embryo,

> I ... find myself driven by the thrust of the biblical material, by theological arguments and by the undeniable reality of widespread human intuitions about abortion, to the conclusion that we owe a duty of protection and care to the embryo and the early fetus as much as to the mature fetus and newborn baby. ... There is no point from fertilisation onwards at which we can reliably conclude that a human being is not a member of the human family, one who is known and called by God, one with whom we are locked in community.[30]

Christ became a member of this community when he began his human life as an embryo. He developed as we all did, so that the speaker we mentioned earlier could say with certainty that this is what Christ looked like as an embryo. It is what we all looked like at that stage, fully human and known by God. Therefore methods of conception or research that lead to the destruction of an embryo can never be acceptable, because when we destroy an embryo, we destroy a fellow human being.

Non-Christian Perspectives: An Overview

Non-Christians have widely differing beliefs about the beginning of human life. At one end of the spectrum, Sikhs and Buddhists believe that human life begins with fertilisation, while, at the other end, members of the Jewish religion hold that the child only gains full human status at birth. Hindus and Muslims believe that the foetus only becomes fully human at some point during pregnancy; Muslims fix this point at about 120 days, while Hindus believe that the foetus becomes a person at a non-specified 'very early stage.'[31] Hinduism therefore forbids IVF. Most non-Christians also advocate extreme caution about the use of embryos for experimentation.[32]

In sum, non-Christian religions which teach that human life begins with conception also normally grant the embryo and foetus the respect due to all human beings.

Conclusion

The Status of the Embryo and Threats to Embryonic Human Life

We have demonstrated that the embryo must be regarded as a full member of the human community, both from a scientific and a religious point of view. In spite of this evidence, the embryo is the least protected of all human beings, with increasing numbers being destroyed throughout the world every year as a result of medical interventions and research.

For anyone who is convinced of the full humanity of the embryo, the obvious question is how to halt this large-scale destruction. This is above all the task of ordinary men and women, as they are the ones for whose potential benefit the techniques that involve embryo destruction have been developed. Governments make decisions, for instance, about the use of weapons of mass destruction, but private individuals decide whether to use IVF or PGD. By refusing to be involved with embryo destruction they can reduce significantly the number of human lives under threat and thereby take responsibility for life and death in a new way.

Overall Summary

- *In Vitro fertilisation* (IVF), *Pre-Implantation Genetic Diagnosis* (PGD) and embryo experimentation are all intended to benefit mankind, but all involve embryo destruction.

- PGD involves the elimination of disease-carrying embryos. Reservations about PGD involve not only the embryo destruction, but the deliberate elimination of sick or handicapped human beings.

- Embryo experimentation involves either using embryos left over from IVF or creating embryos for research only. In both cases the embryos are destroyed once they have served their purpose.

- IVF, PGD and embryo experimentation depend for their acceptability on the belief that the embryo is not a full human being, or else an expendable human being.

- According to the teaching of the Catholic Church and of some other Christians and non-Christians, human life begins with conception and must therefore be respected from then onwards. This teaching agrees with the evidence of contemporary embryological research.

- By refusing to engage in treatments that involve embryo destruction, ordinary people have an unprecedented opportunity to preserve human life.

The one-cell embryo has a blueprint for his or her entire development, so that there is an unbroken continuum from conception to birth and beyond. On that basis alone there are conclusive grounds for treating the embryo with the respect due to a human being, grounds which can be accepted by anyone, whatever their religious or ethical persuasion. If embryos may not be destroyed, then it follows that the foetus in the womb may not be destroyed either. The morality of abortion will be the subject of our next chapter.

Notes

[1]   M. Condic, *When Does Human Life Begin? A Scientific Perspective*, White Paper (New York: Westchester Institute for Ethics & Human Personhood, 2008). www.westchesterinstitute.net/images/wi_whitepaper_life_print.pdf (11 February 2011).

[2]   *Ibid.*, p. 17.

[3]   *Ibid*, pp. 24–25.

[4]   Between 1991 and 2005 the number of treatment cycles for IVF in the UK rose from almost 6000 in 1991 to about 33,500 in 2005. Since half to two thirds of the embryos created were never used, this means an embryo wastage over the period of well over a million. House of Lords Written Answer to Lord Alton of Liverpool, 17 December 2007.

[5]   Department for Transport (2006), 'Road Casualties Great Britain: 2006—Annual Report'.

[6]   Table 4.2, from Centers for Disease Control and Prevention, CDC 2006 Assisted Reproductive Technology (ART) Report, http://www.cdc.gov/art/ART2006/section5.htm (19 January 2011).

[7]   See National Highway Traffic Safety Administration data on https://www-fars.nhtsa.dot.gov/Main/. The estimated embryo deaths are based on the assumption that eight embryos are produced per cycle, with two being implanted and the remaining six wasted. There was a total of 1,152,067 treatment cycles in the US between 1996 and 2006. Multiplied by 6, this equals about seven million. Since not all implanted embryos 'take', this is a conservative estimate.

[8]   A. Murdoch, *The Times*, 24 December 2005.

[9]   M J. Tucker, 'Only a tiny Percentage of Eggs or Embryos Will

Become Babies' *in American Society for Reproductive Medicine: 'Highlights from the 66ᵗʰ Annual Meeting: Humans are Inefficient Reproducers'*, 25 October 2010, http://www.asrm.org/news/article.aspx?id=4643 (24 January 2011).

[10] HFEA press release, 10 May 2006, http://www.hfea.gov.uk/en/1124.html (23 January 2008) and *The Times* 13 May 2006.

[11] *The Times*, 13 May 2006.

[12] *The Times*, 14 November 2006.

[13] http://www.hfea.gov.uk/cps/rde/xchg/SID-3F57D79B-06329BE6/hfea/hs.xsl/385.html (1 November 2006).

[14] HFEA, 'The HFEA Act (and other legislation)', http://www.hfea.gov.uk/134.html (14 February 2011).

[15] Stem Cell Information, National Institutes of Health Guidelines on Human Stem Cell Research', http://stemcells.nih.gov/policy/2009guidelines.htm and 'Stem Cell Information, National Institutes of Health Guidelines on Human Stem Cell Research', http://stemcells.nih.gov/policy/2009guidelines.htm (6 April 2011) and *Advancing Science Serving Society* (AAAS), AAAS Policy Brief: Stem Cell Research, 'The New NIH Guidelines', http://www.aaas.org/spp/cstc/briefs/stemcells/ (6 April 2011).

[16] Article 40.3.3 of the Irish Constitution and report in *The Times*, 16 November 2006.

[17] http://www.womensviewsonnews.org/wvon/2011/03/poll-most-uk-women-would-move-house-for-state-funded-ivf/ (15 April 2011).

[18] K.L. Hudson, 'Preimplantation genetic diagnosis: public policy and public attitudes', in *Fertility and Sterility*, Vol. 85/6 (June 2006), p. 1642. Available via http://www.dnapolicy.org/policy.polls.html?print=1 (13 April 2011).

[19] K.L. Hudson, 'Preimplantation genetic diagnosis: public policy and public attitudes', in *Fertility and Sterility*, Vol. 85/6 (June 2006), p. 1643. Available via http://www.dnapolicy.org/policy.polls.html?print=1 (13 April 2011).

[20] Report of Conference: *The Genetic Town Hall: Making Every Voice Count*, Genetic and Public Policy Center, Washington DC (2004), p. 12, http://www.dnapolicy.org/policy.polls.html?prints=1 (13 April 2011).

[21] Jr 1:4–5.

[22] Lk 1:31–32.

[23] Pope Benedict XVI, *Address to the 12ᵗʰ General Assembly of the*

Pontifical Academy for Life (7 February 2006). Cf. Pope John Paul II, *Evangelium Vitae*, 57. For a detailed discussion of theological opinion about the time creation of the soul, see D. A. Jones, *The Soul of the Embryo* (London: Continuum, 2004) p. 174 and *passim*.

24 Congregation for the Doctrine of the Faith, *Donum Vitae*, I.1.

25 *Catechism of the Catholic Church*, 2270-2271.

26 Catholic Bishops' Conference of England and Wales, *Cherishing Life* (London: Catholic Truth Society and Colloquium (CaTEW) Ltd, 2004) 128.

27 Catholic Bishops' Conference of England and Wales, *Cherishing Life* (London: Catholic Truth Society and Colloquium (CaTEW) Ltd, 2004), 179, quoting John Paul II, *Evangelium Vitae*, 63.

28 Board of Social Responsibility of the Church of England, Report 1985, 118. Reference from http://www.eubios.info/EJ64/EJ64H.htm (11 February 2011).

29 Board of Social Responsibility of the Church of England, Report 1965, 36-45,61. http://www.eubios.info/EJ64/EJ64H.htm (11 February 2011).`

30 J. Wyatt, *Matters of Life and Death*, Today's Healthcare Dilemmas in the Light of the Christian Faith (Leicester: Intervarsity Press, 1998 reprinted 2001), p. 155.

31 'Abortion and Religion', from Education for Choice, www.efc.org.uk (6 May 2010).BBC–religions–Hinduism: Abortion, http://www.bbc.co.uk/ religion/religions/hinduism/hinduethics/abortion_1.shtml (8 July 2010). I. B. Syed, 'Abortion in Islam', http://www.islamawareness.net/FamilyPanning/Abortion/Abortion3.html (6 May 2010). Religious Tolerance.org, 'When does human personhood begin?' Belief system 4: Jewish beliefs, http://www.religioustolerance.org/jud_abor.htm (6 July 2010).

32 R. Beck and D. Worden, *Truth, Spirituality and Contemporary Issues*, (Oxford:Heinemann, 2002), pp. 28–32.

3 THREATS TO HUMAN LIFE: ABORTION

W HEN I WAS a student, I sometimes washed the floors in the maternity ward of a hospital to supplement my grant. I had worked in other wards too, but, in the maternity ward, there was always a sense of joy and never more so than at the actual moment of a birth. Even from my lowly position, washing the floor next door, I could hear the midwife's triumphant shout, 'The baby's coming!' It sounded as if she, too, was having this baby and wanted to share her joy with everyone around.

People of an older generation sometimes speak of a baby as 'a bundle of joy', but joy is not every woman's reaction on finding that she is pregnant. For more and more women today, pregnancy does not lead to the birth of a baby, but to an abortion. Sometimes abortion is carried out for medical reasons, but increasingly it also takes place for what might be called social reasons.

The original motivation for legalising abortion in our times was a desire to avoid the risks of backstreet abortions and also to save the mother's life, if it was in danger due to the pregnancy. However, the legislation of many countries has now been changed so as to make abortion available virtually on demand. A woman's right to choose has become the watchword for claiming easy access to abortion, not only when there is a risk to the mother's life or health, but also when the pregnancy has occurred as an unwanted consequence of sex.

The wish to separate the pleasure of the sexual act from pregnancy is not new. There have always been situations where people have wanted to have sex without the act leading to a pregnancy, and, in the case of an unintended pregnancy, there have always been attempts to induce an abortion. This can be seen, for instance, from the professional oath for doctors formulated around 400 BC by the Greek physician Hippocrates and still sworn by many doctors today. Significantly, it includes a promise not to induce an abortion.[1] Such a promise would have been unnecessary, if abortions had not taken place, even in antiquity. The difference between those times, and indeed the whole of human history before the contraceptive pill was developed, is that it is now possible to avoid pregnancy with a reasonable degree of certainty. However, unplanned pregnancies do occur and, in these cases, abortion often becomes a backstop to contraception. When a handicapped child is aborted, this must be seen as an extension of the destruction of embryos with an inherited disease that we have already described.

In this chapter we will point to the shifts in attitudes which have led to the legalisation of abortion in ever widening circumstances, so that it has become a significant threat to human life. We will show that the desire for an abortion is increasingly motivated by a desire for a perceived good life, which would, it is thought, be blighted by the birth of a child; we will also point to the dangers of using abortion as a means of selecting only the best specimens of the human race. Finally, we will argue for respect for all human life, whether born or unborn, from the moment of conception onwards.

Much of what I will say in this chapter goes against current trends. Nevertheless, I hope that the reader will be convinced by my arguments in favour of granting the unborn child the same right to life as everyone else.

Mother and Unborn Child

A human being comes into existence at conception, so that, when an abortion is considered, there are always two persons involved, the mother and the unborn child. The mother can speak for herself and can put forward arguments for having an abortion. The child, however, has no voice and can only influence others indirectly. Hence there is a need to consider carefully the balance between the rights of the mother and those of the unborn child. In normal circumstances, no one doubts the fact that a grown woman is a human being who has the right to life. On the other hand, there is much uncertainty, both in law and the minds of individuals, about the rights of the foetus.

There are many reasons for this, but the most prominent one is the much-vaunted 'right to choose' of the mother. If the right to life of the child is to be respected, the mother needs to accept him or her. On the other hand, if she chooses to have an abortion, then the child will die and that is when the rights of the mother and the unborn child come into conflict.

The ambiguity about the rights of the foetus is revealed in the way pregnancy loss is reported under different circumstances. For instance, the expression, 'She lost her unborn baby', is often used about a wanted child, whereas, 'She needed an abortion,' refers to the destruction of a foetus who is either unwanted or considered too handicapped or sick to have a life worth living. In the first case, the foetus is an 'unborn baby', whereas, in the second case, the foetus is referred to only by implication, as the cause of the woman 'needing an abortion.' Nevertheless, the foetus does have some rights.

The Rights of the Unborn Child

As we have seen, every human being begins life as an embryo. Since the embryo is a human being from the moment of conception, it follows that the foetus is a human being too. The foetus should therefore be entitled to the rights of all human beings. Unfortunately this is rarely so.

Much legislation about the rights of the foetus suffers from a bad case of split personality. In some countries the unborn child is granted specific legal rights, but, in most cases, these rights do not prevent abortion from taking place, regardless of foetal rights. The most absolute right to life of the unborn child was, until recently, enshrined in the Irish Constitution, but, since 2013, Irish legislation has been changed so as to permit an abortion if the mother's life is in danger. In 2018 the protection of the unborn child was further weakened so as to allow abortions during the early stages of pregnancy in other cases as well.

In the UK, abortion is illegal, but the law does not grant the foetus an independent right to life; it only forbids others to abort the child. However, the *Abortion Act* of 1967 permits so many exceptions to the law that, in practice, the foetus has almost no legal protection.[2]

In the US, the *Unborn Victims of Violence Act* (2004) defines violent assault against a pregnant woman as a crime against two persons: the woman and the foetus, so that in such cases the foetus is recognised as a person against whom a crime can be committed. However, since the *Act* specifically excludes prosecution for a legal abortion, it does not protect the unborn child in all circumstances.[3]

It is as if many legislators think about the foetus in two separate boxes. In one, they see an unborn child who must be protected, while, in the other, they see the same child as an obstacle to the mother's wishes. They fail to see that there are two human beings, both of whom have the right to life. Instead, they let the right to choose of the mother override the right to life of the unborn child.

Why is there a Demand for Abortion?

Panic is often a woman's first reaction on discovering an unexpected and unwanted pregnancy. In the past, society did not look kindly on an unmarried mother. If the father did not want to marry her, or could not, because he was already married, she was indeed in a desperate situation. She would become an outcast, a 'fallen woman' and 'no better than she should be.' In such circumstances, even her parents would sometimes abandon her. It is therefore not surprising that, in her desperation, she might turn to illegal means of ending the pregnancy. For most women, the only way of doing so was through a backstreet abortion, which would often leave her permanently injured. Some of these abortions even led to the death of the woman.

There were other reasons, too, for an increasing call for legal abortions in the UK. These related to cases where a woman had become pregnant after rape, where her life was in danger due to the pregnancy or where she was carrying a seriously malformed infant. As we shall see, the reaction to some of these extreme cases has paved the way to a wider access to legal abortion. However, hard cases often make bad law.

In recent years, there has been a shift in many women's motivation for wanting an abortion from fear of condemnation and social exclusion to a desire to avoid financial problems and on to a regretful decision to abort a child, because the father was no longer in the picture. Some women now consider abortion simply as a necessary procedure to end an unwanted pregnancy. This last motivation has led inexorably towards a campaign to legalise abortion on demand. We will now look at how abortion legislation has developed in the UK and the US.

Abortion Legislation in the UK

In the UK abortion has been prohibited in law since the Middle Ages. Even today, when a large number of abortions take place, these are performed as exceptions to the legal prohibition. However, the number of exceptions has increased dramatically, especially in the last fifty years. It is therefore possible to trace a development from no exceptions permitted, to a few exceptions, to so many exceptions that, in practice, there is now abortion on demand in the UK. How has this development come about? Let us take as our starting point the *Offences against the Person Act* of 1861 which made abortion a criminal offence carrying a maximum sentence of penal servitude for life. Here the focus was on punishing those who performed an abortion rather than the unborn child.

With the *Infant Life Preservation Act* of 1929 the focus changed. The purpose of this Act was to protect the life of the infant in the womb, rather than to punish those who attacked it. Nevertheless, the Act did allow an abortion in cases where the mother's life was in danger, but only up to twenty eight weeks of pregnancy. After that the child was deemed to be 'capable of being born alive' and therefore could not be legally aborted. Nevertheless there was a significant change in attitude from the previous Act, because abortion was allowed in some very limited cases, though never after viability. This changed with the abortion legislation of 1967.

However, even before 1967, there was an important development in the interpretation of the 1929 Act. The Act had granted permission for an abortion only if the pregnancy was a physical threat to the mother's life. A threat to her mental health was not considered grounds for an abortion. That interpretation of the law was challenged in 1938 when a young woman became pregnant after a gang rape by a group of soldiers. The respected gynaecologist Dr Aleck Bourne agreed to perform an abortion, because, in his opinion, the woman would be left a mental wreck, if she was forced to go through with the pregnancy. He was prosecuted, but found not guilty of performing an illegal abortion and the case set a legal precedent for allowing abortion on mental health grounds.

The legal ruling in this extreme case had unforeseen consequences. To Dr Bourne's dismay, the number of abortions on mental health grounds increased steadily in the years that followed. By the mid-1960s he was so concerned at what he considered to be a gross misuse of psychiatric medicine that he helped to found the *Society for the Protection of Unborn Children* (SPUC) in order to prevent the1966 Abortion Bill from becoming law.[4] Nevertheless, the Bill became law in 1967.

Although the number of abortions increased during the years between the Bourne case and the 1967 *Abortion Act*, most legal abortions were performed privately for wealthy women, while poorer women tended to resort to so-called backstreet abortions. The intention of the new legislation was to provide legal means for women in crisis pregnancies to have an abortion and also to enable doctors to perform these without fear of prosecution.

Basically, the 1967 Act allowed abortion before twenty eight weeks, if there was a risk to the mother's physical or mental health or to the physical or mental health of existing children or family members. The last two grounds, which are sometimes called the social grounds, are often very widely interpreted. The Act also allowed abortions after twenty eight weeks, if there was a risk to the life of the mother or if there was a risk that the child would be born with a serious physical or mental handicap.

During the years following the *Abortion Act*, there were significant advances in the care of very premature babies. This meant that some babies born at twenty four weeks were now able to survive. Because of this, there was an amendment to the *Act* in 1990, which restricted abortion after twenty four weeks. However, the same amendment also legalised abortion up to full term if the baby was seriously handicapped or there was a serious threat to the mother's life or health.[5] This meant that, in the same hospital, doctors could now be trying to save the life of a twenty-four-week baby in one ward, while, in another, they would regretfully be ending the life of a handicapped baby of the same number of weeks.

UK abortion figures in the forty years between 1969 and 2010 reveal how much the practice of abortion has increased. During this period the number of legal abortions per year in England and Wales rose from about 55,000 in 1969 to about 200,000 in 2010, with a peak of about 205,600 in 2007. This means that, over the forty-year period, the number of abortions per year in just one country had roughly quadrupled.[6]

The year 2007 saw the fortieth anniversary of the *Abortion Act*. On this occasion, David Steel, the MP who had originally introduced the *Abortion Bill*, gave an interview which threw revealing light on the change of mindset in the population over those four decades. He said that he had never thought that there would be so many abortions and that, in his view, abortion had come to be used as a form of contraception.[7]

The following examples illustrate how widely the *Abortion Act* had come to be interpreted.

Unborn Child with Harelip

As we have seen, the law in the UK now permits abortions after twenty four weeks, if the child is found to have a serious handicap. However, it is not easy to define what is meant by serious handicap, as one person's serious handicap can be another person's minor handicap. In the parliamentary debate in 1990 about a revision of the *Abortion Act*, the possibility of interpreting 'serious' to include, for instance, babies with harelip, was raised. At the time, this objection was rejected by a supporter of the Act, who said that such a suggestion was 'pure scaremongering, which is appalling.'[8]

However, some ten years later, a Church of England curate, Joanna Jepson, discovered that a late abortion had been carried out precisely for this 'scaremongering' reason.[9] She had herself been born with a harelip which had later been corrected, so she knew from personal experience that this condition could be treated. The High Court gave her permission to challenge the legality of this abortion through a judicial review.[10] The review was later abandoned when the police authority in whose area the 'harelip' abortion had taken place decided to review the case to see if there were grounds for a criminal prosecution. The outcome of the inquiry was that there were insufficient grounds for prosecuting the two doctors involved. Commenting on the case, the Chief Crown Prosecutor for the area said that the doctors had carried out the abortion in good faith, believing that the child would be seriously handicapped.[11]

This interpretation is not an isolated instance, because in 2011 the government released figures showing that, in the previous nine years, there had been twenty six abortions on the grounds of harelip or cleft palate. In response to this information, Miss Jepson wrote an article warning of the danger that society would come to regard all handicapped children in the womb as unfit to be born.[12]

Not ready for a Child

When a woman wants an abortion, two doctors have to agree that she fulfils the legal conditions for the abortion. In one case, which I know of, the reasons for the termination were the shortness of the patient's relationship with the child's father combined with her concerns about the effect of a child on her career. In short, the woman did not feel ready for a baby either from a relationship or from a career point of view. As these grounds do not fall within the law and as no physical grounds were mentioned in connection with the case, I can only assume that the abortion was performed on the basis of a risk to the mental health of the patient.[13]

Abortion Legislation in the US

Abortion legislation in the US has had a chequered history, which is complicated by the fact that individual states have their own laws. Before the 1820s, abortion was legal throughout the US up to the time of quickening, that is, when the mother first felt the unborn child move. However, in the course of the nineteenth century an increasing number of states prohibited abortion at any time, except when the pregnant woman's life was in danger. This prohibition roughly agreed with UK legislation of the same period.

The picture in the US changed dramatically in 1973 after a court case often referred to as the Roe v Wade case. The dispute was between a woman who claimed the right to an abortion and the State of Texas which sought to defend its anti-abortion laws. The names *Roe* and *Wade* were pseudonyms referring to the woman and the attorney for the State of Texas respectively. The case was eventually referred to the US Supreme Court, which ruled that the Texas anti-abortion laws violated a woman's right to privacy; this meant that the laws went against her right to decide whether or not to terminate a pregnancy.

However, the Supreme Court recognised three competing sets of rights to be protected: the woman's right to privacy, the government's right to protect the health of the woman and finally the government's right to protect the health of the unborn child. The court ruled that, during the first three months, the decision to abort could be made by the woman in consultation with her physician. During the next three months, individual states could restrict abortion to some extent, while, during the last three months, they were free to forbid all abortions, except when the woman's life was in danger.[14]

Basically, the Supreme Court had sought to protect a woman's right to an abortion throughout her pregnancy, at least if her life was in danger. At the same time it removed any legal protection for the unborn child during the early stages of pregnancy, leaving only limited protection during the later stages.

After the Roe v Wade ruling, a further legal difficulty arose, because the US constitution requires that no state 'shall deprive any person of life.'[15] If the foetus was considered a person in law, then the ruling would have been unconstitutional. In order to avoid this difficulty, the court decided that the foetus was not a person in law.

However, when an unborn child is a victim of violence, for instance in a car accident, the law does consider the child a 'person' with the rights of a person. So as not to invalidate abortion legislation, the relevant legal Act states that nothing in it can lead to the prosecution of anyone in relation to an abortion to which the pregnant woman has consented.[16]

Taken together, these laws and rulings mean that an unborn child is a 'person', if a victim of violence, but is not a person, if the mother chooses to abort it. As in a number of other countries, the laws concerning the rights of the unborn child in the US are mutually contradictory.

Since the Roe v Wade case, the number of abortions annually in the US have risen steadily until 1990, after which there has been a noticeable decline. Thus in 1973 there were almost 700,000 legal abortions, rising to a high of over 1.5 million in 1990. By 2006 the total had dropped to less than 1.25 million, which may have been due to more efficient use of contraceptives combined with a greater willingness among some women to carry an unintended pregnancy to term.[17] If the latter is true, then that is a development in the right direction.

UK and US Abortions Compared with Second World War Deaths

Since abortion was made legal in 1967, there has been a total of over seven million abortions in the UK, which comes to seventy times the number of people killed in the Hiroshima and Nagasaki bombings in Japan during the Second World War.[18] In the US the total of known abortions since the Roe v Wade Case in 1973 comes to approximately forty million or four hundred times the combined number of people killed in the atomic bombings in Japan.[19] What is more, if the number of known embryo and abortion deaths in the UK are added to those of the US, the total comes to at least sixty million, which is the same as all the military and civilian deaths in the Second World War.[20] This is the scale of death before birth in our times in the UK and the US alone.

How has this been allowed to happen? It is very largely because the embryo and the foetus, the human being before birth, is not consistently recognised as such.

Part of US legislation has acknowledged that the child in the womb is a human being, because, when a pregnant woman is injured, the law speaks of two 'persons' being injured. However, this has not prevented the advent of legal abortion. This contradiction within the law reflects a contradiction in many people's attitude to the unborn child. The child who is wanted must be saved at all costs, but the child who is not wanted, or considered too handicapped, can be aborted.

Legislation does not happen in a vacuum. In a democracy, laws tend to reflect the opinions of the majority. Let us therefore look at the results of some recent opinion polls on abortion in the UK, the US and Ireland.

Public Opinion about Abortion in the UK, the US and Ireland

Opinion polls are not infallible, but they can give a feel for how the basic attitudes of ordinary people have shifted over time.

UK

In the UK there are very few opinion polls about abortion, but those that exist show that a majority of people think abortion should be legal, or mostly legal. In one of the polls available, the majority in favour of access to termination was well over half; in another, about three quarters were in favour.

Because of the Catholic Church's teaching that abortion is never justified, it might be assumed that a poll of Catholics on this subject would show a different view to the population at large. Surprisingly, a recent poll aimed solely at Catholics revealed that a majority were in favour of access to abortion, at least in some cases. Nine out of ten approved of abortion if a woman had been raped and thirteen out of fourteen agreed that a termination should be legal, if a woman's health was in danger.[21] On a basis of this poll, it seems that many Catholics hold opinions about abortion that are not radically different to those of the rest of the population and that therefore differ from the official teaching of the Catholic Church. On the other hand, the poll only referred to the most extreme situations in which abortion might be considered. If it had covered a wider range of cases, I suspect that there might have been significant differences between the opinion of most Catholics and those of the majority of the population.

US

In the US, the Gallup organisation has taken an annual poll of attitudes to abortion since 1976, so that there is far more information available than for the UK. For the period from 1976 to 2010, the polls show that roughly fifty per cent of those questioned were consistently in favour of legal abortion in special circumstances. However, figures for those in favour of abortion on demand and those totally against have varied considerably up to the year 2000. Since then, the two groups at the extreme ends of the spectrum have been roughly equal at around twenty per cent each.

In response to the question, 'Do you consider yourself pro-choice or pro-life?' those in favour of each stance have been approximately equal for the last fifteen years. This means that attitudes to the right to life of the unborn child are far more evenly balanced and therefore more polarised in the US than in the UK.[22]

Ireland

Ireland is one the countries where Catholic teaching, at least until recently, strongly influenced attitudes to the rights of the unborn child. This was revealed particularly clearly in the result of a referendum on the right to life of the unborn, held in 1983. In this large-scale poll, an overwhelming majority of the population voted in favour of enshrining the right to life of the unborn child in the Irish Constitution. As a result, an amendment was added, acknowledging this right.[23]

However, in 2013 a new law was passed, which permits an abortion if the woman's life is thought to be at risk due to the pregnancy. Though this law is not the result of a referendum, it reflects a change in attitude to abortion in the Irish population in the past thirty years. There is a vociferous pro-choice lobby in Ireland and, over recent years, many women have travelled to England for an abortion. These developments show that, even in a pre-dominantly Catholic country such as Ireland, an increasing number of people no longer believe that the unborn child always has the right to life.[24]

This change was confirmed by the result of a new referendum in 2018, which revealed an almost two thirds majority in favour of a further relaxation of Irish abortion law, so as to permit the abortion of an unborn child during the first twelve weeks of pregnancy and also up to twenty four weeks in some circumstances.

The Voice of the Unborn Child

Those who Might have been Aborted Speak out

When a handicapped unborn child is aborted, this is based on the assumption that he or she would not have wanted to live. Many disabled people have spoken out against this assumption and their voices are the closest we can get to hearing the voice of the unborn child. The following two examples are typical of the attitude of many handicapped people.

Some years ago I watched a programme about thalidomide victims who had grown to adulthood. I found the comments of one young woman who had been born without arms particularly moving. When the interviewer asked her whether she thought she should have been aborted, she said that everyone must be given their chance in life and that she certainly did not wish that her life had been cut short in the womb. She then took the camera crew to her trampoline, where she jumped up and down with such joy that no one could doubt that she was indeed grateful for her life.

Christy Nolan is a severely handicapped man who was awarded the Whitbread Book of the Year prize in 1987 for his autobiography *Under the Eye of the Clock*, in which he spoke up not just for his own right to life, but that of all handicapped people. He typed the whole book with the aid of a unicorn stick attached to his forehead but, as he was unable to speak, his mother read his acceptance speech for him. This is what he said,

> You all must realize that history is in the making. Tonight a crippled man is taking his place on the world literary stage. Tonight is my night for laughing, for crying tears of joy. But wait, my brothers hobble after me hinting. What about silent us? Can

we too have a voice? Tonight I am speaking for
them ... imagine what I would have missed if the
doctors had not revived me on that September day
long ago ... Can *yessing* be so difficult that, rather
than give a baby a chance of life, man treads upon
his brother and silences him before he can draw
one breath of this world's fresh air?[25]

After he was born, Nolan was very nearly left to die,
because the doctors did not think it worthwhile reviving
such a severely handicapped child. Although the action,
or rather inaction, in Nolan's case would not technically
have been an abortion, the principle of not considering a
handicapped life worth preserving is the same.

It is, of course, true that there are handicapped and sick
people who do not wish to live—and we will return to this
question in a later chapter—but it cannot be assumed that,
had they been given the choice, everyone with a severe
handicap would have chosen not to be born.

Christianity and Abortion

It might be assumed that denominations which teach that
human life begins with conception would also teach that
the right to life begins at that point, so that they would
never allow abortion. However, the situation is not as
simple as that. Just as, in law, the life of the human being
is protected from conception onwards in some cases, but
not in others, so, in some Christian churches, the right to
life of the embryo and unborn child is protected in some
instances, but not in others. Some denominations therefore face the same conflict between the rights of the
mother or parents and the rights of the embryo and foetus
as does contemporary legislation.

As we saw in the previous chapter, the Catholic Church
has always taught that the human being comes into

existence at conception and a number of other Christians agree with this. In addition there are people of no religion who hold similar views. On the other hand, there are Christians who believe that the full human person, with body and soul, does not begin to exist till later on in pregnancy. This conviction makes it possible for them to accept the embryo destruction associated with IVF and also to allow some abortions. In what follows, the phrases *human being* and *human person* are used interchangeably.

Christian Views on the Right to Life and Abortion

Although Scripture does not speak explicitly of abortion, it does forbid the taking of innocent human life.[26] Since the person, according to Scripture, begins with conception, the commandment not to kill applies as much to the human being before as after birth.

With reference to the effect of legislation permitting abortion, a Catholic teaching document states poignantly that, once a particular law has deprived a whole category of human beings of legal protection, the state has denied the equality of everyone before the law.[27] The Catholic Church therefore asserts the right to life of every human person from conception onwards, which is implied in the UN *Declaration of Human Rights,* but often contradicted in national legislation.

The weakening of the rights of the foetus can also be seen in the teaching of some non-Catholic Christian denominations. For instance, at synods in 1983 and 1993, the Church of England accepted the view that, if an unborn child was seriously disabled or the mother's life was in danger, an abortion could be justified.[28] This contradicted the statement of an earlier synod that the foetus had the right to life and that abortion was 'a great moral evil'.[29] Thus, although the Church of England recognises the right to life of the foetus, it no longer believes that this right is absolute.

The Orthodox Churches believe that abortion can only be justified if the life of the mother is at risk, so that, unlike the Anglican Church, they do not permit the abortion of a seriously handicapped child. Many Evangelical Christians are totally opposed to abortion, although the Methodist Church leaves the decision to individual women.[30]

As we can see, there is a wide range of beliefs about the morality of abortion within non-Catholic Christian churches, leading to a conflict between recognition of the right to life of the unborn child and acceptance of abortion in some cases.

Non-Christian Religions: An Overview

Non-Christian religions have a range of different views on the morality of abortion. For instance, Hindus generally consider abortion wrong, except to save the mother's life. However, because of a cultural preference for sons, female infants are sometimes aborted.[31]

There are various schools of thought about the morality of abortion within Islam, but, in general, it is considered wrong except to save the mother's life.[32]

Judaism has a range of teachings on the acceptability of abortion. It is permitted to save the mother's life and sometimes in other cases after consultation between the mother, her husband, her doctor and her rabbi. According to some, the decision should be made on a case-by-case basis by a rabbi well versed in Jewish law.[33]

According to some Buddhists, abortion is an act of killing and therefore forbidden, but others say that it can be permissible if carried out with compassion for the

mother or for a seriously handicapped infant. The Dalai
Lama has made the following telling comment,

> Of course, abortion, from a Buddhist viewpoint, is
> an act of killing and is negative, generally speaking.
> ... But it depends on the circumstances ... I think
> abortion should be approved or disapproved
> according to each circumstance.[34]

These words neatly sum up the attitudes to abortion both
of civil society and of many religions and individuals.
Basically, he is saying that killing, including the killing of
an unborn child, is wrong, but that, nevertheless, there can
be circumstances in which it is defensible to take the life
of such a child. Thus the right to life of a human person
before birth is made conditional on the circumstances, so
that respect for the life of child comes to depend entirely
on the subjective choice of those in charge of him or her.

A Woman's Right to Choose

When a woman discovers that she is unexpectedly pregnant, it is widely believed that she a has a right to choose
whether to carry on with the pregnancy or not. Often the
child is seen as an unfortunate consequence of an act of sex;
she was unlucky and now needs a remedy for her problem.
However, unless she has been raped, she had a choice when
she decided to have sex when she was neither able nor
willing to care for the child that might be the result.

At its best, the act of love is a gift between a man and a
woman who are committed to each other and who are
prepared to bring up together the child they might conceive. The child is then not seen as a threat to be removed
if necessary, but as a person to be respected and cherished.

However, even in these circumstances, some people
would advocate an abortion, if the pregnancy turns out to

pose a serious medical threat to the mother's health or life. When the child she is expecting is found to be seriously handicapped, the mother is also often urged to have an abortion.

Hard Cases

When discussing the Catholic Church's teaching on abortion, I have often come across the comment, 'No one who has not been in a crisis pregnancy can possibly know what it's like or what they would do.' The right to life of the unborn child becomes real in a new way to a woman in such a situation. Nevertheless, I believe that even people like myself who have not had such a pregnancy can reflect on some of the hard cases that are frequently mentioned in support of a wider right to abortion.

Mother's Life in Danger

In a recent newspaper article on abortion the writer began by saying that she was 'pro-life', 'the life of the mother', thereby implying that abortion was mostly carried out to save the life of the pregnant woman. In fact, the mother's life is very rarely under threat. For instance, in 2010 less than one per cent of all abortions in the UK were carried out because the mother's life was in danger.[35] Thus the strongly emotive argument that abortion is often necessary to save the life of the mother does not reflect the reality of most abortions. What is more, even if a woman's life is threatened, modern medical methods can nearly always enable her to continue till the twenty-fourth or twenty-fifth week, that is, till her baby is viable and can be safely delivered. In this way both mother and child are given a good chance of survival.[36]

Disabled Child

It is often assumed that, if a handicapped child could have been asked, he or she would have preferred not to be born. However, many handicapped people have spoken out vigorously against this assumption; as we have seen, the young woman who was disabled by thalidomide and the author Christy Nolan who was nearly left to die at birth were both grateful for the chance to live. It is true that not all handicapped people are thankful that they were not aborted, but at least they were given a chance to make something of their lives. When people destroy a life, they give in to despair; when they save it, on the other hand, they look to the future with hope and we will return to these topics in a later chapter.

Rape Victim

Of all the hard cases one could think of, the woman who has become pregnant after rape is surely the hardest and the one that calls for most compassion. The thought of carrying the child of the man who has violated her must, to begin with at least, fill her with revulsion. Pope Francis has spoken of the need to accompany women in such a situation, where an abortion may seem 'a quick solution to her profound anguish'.[37] Yet an abortion would be a further act of violence against an innocent human being.

If a woman is to make the heroic decision to continue with the pregnancy, she will need much support, from her family, from health services and from her faith community. Having decided against abortion, she then has the further decision of whether to keep the child or have it adopted. Here different women will react differently, and much will depend on their circumstances, both financial and social.

In my personal opinion, adoption would probably be the best choice, as this would mean that both the child and the mother would start with a clean slate.

However, it would not be everyone's choice. For some women the fact that the child was partly hers would weigh heavily, so that they might find adoption hard to bear. In this difficult, and fortunately rare, situation, there can be no rights and wrongs about what arrangements to make, as long as the child is given a chance to live.

Conclusion: The Threat to Human Life through Abortion

In connection with every abortion there are two sets of rights: those of the unborn child and those of the mother; the latter are normally at the forefront of any decision, while the former are much less respected.

The tide towards ever greater access to abortion, and hence the threat to the life of the unborn child, can be seen most disturbingly through the fact that the number of abortions taking place every year in the UK and US alone are several hundred times the combined deaths in the Hiroshima and Nagasaki bombings. A woman's 'right to choose' has become her right to choose the death of the child she is carrying.

However, some recent cases of assault on pregnant women in the UK have pointed to a shift in attitudes to the unborn child. The lawyer for one woman, who lost the child she was expecting following an attack, pointed out that the assailant could not be charged with harming the child, because, at present, the child was not considered a *person* in law. In his opinion, there ought to be a new law aimed specifically at people who 'recklessly' kill an unborn baby, which would be similar to the US law we described earlier. In other words, the child ought to be recognised as a *person*, at least if he or she was assaulted! However, if the unborn child was a *person*, when attacked, then surely all unborn children must be *persons*. They cannot be *persons* for some purposes and not for others.[38]

If the threat to the life of the unborn child is to be removed, this can only be done by acknowledging that the child has the same right to life as the mother, since they are both human beings.

Once a woman has taken that truth to heart, she will know that she cannot in conscience abort the child, even though the law permits her to do so. Such a decision may be hard and it will go against the current tide of opinion, but it will in the end lead to the joy of having saved a human life.

Overall Summary

- The loss of unborn human life today is comparable to the total of civilian and military deaths in the Second World War.
- Changes in legislation to permit abortion are driven partly by shifts in public opinion, partly by rulings in landmark court cases.
- The law tends to protect the wanted child, but not the unwanted child and the seriously handicapped child.
- The right to life of the unborn is based on the scientific and religious truth about when human life begins.
- The Catholic Church and some evangelicals are almost alone in defending the right to life of the unborn unconditionally.

The fate of the unborn child is in the hands of ordinary people and above all ordinary women. If they accept the truth about the humanity of the unborn child with his or her inalienable right to life, then there is a possibility of limiting, if not eliminating, the threat to such children. The truth is also the only reliable guide for decisions about the end of life, which will be the subject of the next chapter.

Notes

1   J. Wyatt, *Matters of Life and Death* (Leicester: Intervarsity Press, 1998), p. 215.
2   'The UK Statute Law Database', Abortion Act 1967 (c. 87.1). Available at http://www.statutelaw.gov.uk ,(29 March 2011).
3   *Unborn Victims of Violence Act of 2004* (Public Law 108-212).
4   https://www.spuc.org.uk/about/history (22 August 2014).
5   I mainly follow Wyatt, *Matters of Life and Death*, p. 126ff.
6   Figures available from www.statistics.gov.uk (29 June 2011)
7   As reported in *The Guardian* 24 October 2007.
8   Labour MP Frank Doran, as recorded in *Hansard*. Report *in The Tablet* 29 November 2003.
9   The abortion took place after the twenty four week legal limit for an abortion on grounds other than 'serious handicap' of the foetus. See http://newsvote.bbc.co.uk/mpapps/pagetools/print/news.bbc.co.uk/1/hi/healthy/3247916.stm
10 *The Tablet* 29 November 2003 and http://www.ethicsforschools. org/news/abortion.htm, a site run by the Christian Medical Fellowship. (6 December 2006).
11 As quoted in *BioPortfolio News*, http://www.bioportfolio.com/ march_05/21_03_2005/Fury_as_abortion_doctors.html (8 December 2006).
12 *The Daily Telegraph* 9 July 2011.
13 Termination of pregnancy (TOP) consultation form with identifying details blanked out, as seen by the author.
14 BBC News, http://news.bbc.co.uk/1/hi/world/americas/ 49315.stm (14 December 2010).
15 US Constitution, Fourteenth Amendment, http://topics.law.cornell.edu/ constitution/amendmentxiv (26 July 2011).See also, M. Kogan, 'Roe v. Wade: A simple Explanation of the Most Important SCOTUS Decision in 40 Years', http://www.policymic.com/articles.23822/roe-v-wade-a-

simple-explanation. (19 November 2013).

[16]   United States Code, Section 1841. Protection of unborn children (2) (C)c.

[17]   N. Gibbs, 'Why Have Abortion Rates Fallen?', *in Time*, 21 January 2008.

[18]   Abortion Figures available from www.statistics.gov.uk. (29 June 2011),For atomic bombings, see, 'The Atomic Bombings of Hiroshima and Nagasaki', http://www.atomicarchive.com/ Docs/MED/med_chp10.shtml (21 March 2011).

[19]   Figure based on National Center for Disease Control and Alan Guttmacher Institute figures, *in* 'Christian Life Resources', http://www.christianliferesources.com/?5511 (25 July 2011).

[20]   http://www.historylearningsite.co.uk/military_casualties_ of_world_war.htm. (21 November 2013).

[21]   2010 poll reported in the *Independent on Sunday*, 19 September 2010.

[22]   http://www.gallup.com/poll/1576/abortion.aspx?version=print (27 July 2011).

[23]   Eighth Amendment of the Irish Constitution, as quoted *in* 'Ireland, Abortion Policy' UN website on population, http://www.un.org/esa/population/publications/abortion/doc/ , then go to 'Ireland'. (28 May 2011).

[24]   For an overview of Irish legislation on the right to life of the foetus and on abortion, see C. Gearty, 'Layers of Conflicting Truths' *in The Tablet* 19 October 2013, p. 8.

[25]   As quoted by J. Wyatt, *Matters of life and Death, Today's Health Care Dilemmas in the Light of the Christian Faith*, (Leicester:Intervarsity Press, 1998), p. 105f.

[26]   Ex 20:13 and Dt 5:17.

[27]   Congregation for the Doctrine of the Faith, *Donum Vitae* , III.

[28]   http://www.bbc.co.uk/religion/religions/christianity/ christianethics/abortion_1shtml (10 August 2011).

[29]   Synods 1983 and 1993. As quoted on the BBC website http://www.bbc.co.uk/religion/religions/christianity/christianet hics/abortion_1shtml (10 August 2011).

[30]   *Education for Choice*, www.efc.org.uk (6 May 2010).

[31]   http://www.bbc.co.uk/religion/religions/hinduism/hinduethics /abortion_1.shtml (8 July 2010).

[32]   http://www.bbc.co.uk/religion/religions/islam/islamethics /abortion_print.html (20 October 2009).

[33] http://www.religioustolerance.org/jud_abor.htm (6 July 2010).

[34] As quoted *in* The New York times, 28 November 1993. See also http://www.bbc.co.uk/religion/religions/buddhism/buddhisteth ics/abortion.shtml (8 July 2010).

[35] *Abortion Review* 24 May 2011, 'Statistics for Briefing' (3): Grounds for abortion. http://www.abortionreview.org/index.php /site/article/963/ (17 August 2011).

[36] J. Wyatt, *Matters of Life and Death, Today's healthcare dilemmas in the light of the Christian faith,* (Leicester:Intervarsity Press, 1998), p. 156.

[37] Pope Francis, *Evangelii Gaudium,* 214.

[38] BBC News 17 April 2015, http://www.bbc.co.uk/newsbeat/ article/32332040/why-its-not-murder-to-kill-an-unborn-child (17 April 2015).

4 THREATS TO HUMAN LIFE: ASSISTED SUICIDE AND EUTHANASIA

I N A TELEVISED interview from her hospice bed, shortly before she died, the right-to-die campaigner Debbie Purdy said that she did not want her life to be 'like this'. She had suffered from multiple sclerosis for many years and during that time had campaigned for the right to be helped to die, if her life became unbearable.[1]

She had put into words what many people feel; that there can come a point when they are suffering so much that they see death as the only way out of their pain. If they are not able to commit suicide, they therefore want someone else to help them to die. Effectively, they are saying that they have a right to die, if they so choose. In a growing number of countries, their wish can be legally granted, which means that there is now an increasing threat to human life before its natural end. This threat is based on the belief that serious suffering and a good life are incompatible.

A recent report by a senior British judge recommended that terminally ill people with less than a year to live should be given the legal right to assisted suicide. The newspaper which published details of the report strongly supported the judge's conclusions in its leader, stating that individuals should be allowed 'sovereignty over their own futures' as 'something that [was] rightly theirs'.[2] Here we see one answer to the central question posed by this book, 'Who is in charge of human life, God or man?' According to the paper, men and women had both the right and the ability to take on such a responsibility.

Because they have free will, people certainly have the ability to assume control of their lives, but then they must also take the consequences. In the account of the Fall, when Adam and Eve made such an attempt, the result was conflict and mistrust among people. They could destroy each other's lives, but they could not re-create the harmony and the respect for all human life that had existed before the Fall.

The mistrust among people can be seen, for instance, in the fact that an association of elderly and handicapped people in Holland has now begun to issue its members with a card requesting that the bearer should not be euthanised if admitted to hospital.[3] Here we see the spectre of fear that, once individuals have the right to control the moment of death, that control can also be taken away; they may be put to death against their wishes.

In spite of these warning bells, assisted suicide and euthanasia have now been legalised or at least tacitly accepted in many countries. As we shall see, changes in legislation have been driven by changes in public opinion as well as high profile court cases. Since medical personnel will often be required to assist with the ending of a human life, opinion polls of doctors form an indispensable aspect of our discussion. Finally, it is important to stress that these are not matters for experts only, but questions that each one of us may one day have to consider either for ourselves or for someone close to us.

'I don't Want Life to Be like this': The Demand for Assisted Dying

On a long-distance rail journey I once got talking to the man sitting next to me. Somehow the conversation turned to euthanasia and he said, without any hesitation, that he and his sisters had helped his mother 'across' as he put it, with the help of some extra painkillers from the doctor. 'And', he added, 'when my time comes, I hope someone will do the same for me.'

With these words he had neatly summed up the attitude of many people to assisted suicide and euthanasia today. If they are in too much pain, they want the option of release from suffering by choosing to die. In a similar way, there is now pressure in some cases to allow people in a Persistent Vegetative State (PVS) to die by withdrawing food and water. These opinions are based on the conviction that life is only worth living under certain circumstances.

Attitudes like those of my travel companion have led to changes in legislation in many countries in the West.

Assisted Suicide and Euthanasia

Legislation in the UK, the US and the Netherlands

Both in the UK and in the US legislation is split into two types distinguishing between those with mental capacity and those without, while the Netherlands does not make this distinction. In order to show how legislation has changed in these three countries over the years, we need to provide some detail about the law in each country, beginning with the UK.

UK

Both assisted suicide and euthanasia are illegal in the UK and there are no exceptions to this rule. Thus the law about helping someone to die differs from the ban on abortion, which allows for a wide range of exceptions. However, over the years, the courts have shown increasing leniency towards relatives and friends who, at the patient's request, help him or her to die. Developments in the attitude of the courts towards assisted suicide can best be illustrated through some landmark court cases. In each of these, the motivations both of the patient and of the person assisting with the death were crucial to the verdicts of the court.

The tension between upholding the law and showing sympathy for people in extreme circumstances can be seen in the case of David March, who had helped his disabled wife commit suicide in 2006. He was initially charged with murder, though the charge was later changed to that of assisting someone to commit suicide. During the trial, it emerged that Mrs March, who had suffered from multiple sclerosis for twenty years, had tried to commit suicide on two previous occasions, but her husband had found her and called for help to resuscitate her. When he found her with a plastic bag over her head on a third occasion, he could no longer bear to see her suffer and helped her to die.

Significantly, during his summing-up, the judge said that Mrs March had been determined to 'control 'and then end her life, so that, in his view, David March had no choice but to respect her will.[4] Two things are striking about the judge's comments. Firstly, he spoke of Mrs March taking 'control' of her life. Secondly, the judge said that Mr March had had 'no choice', almost as if he had had an obligation to help his wife to die. For these reasons, Mr March was only given a nine month suspended sentence.

A new development took place in 2010, when the multiple sclerosis sufferer Debbie Purdy sought reassurance from the Director of Public Prosecutions that, in the event of her husband helping her to die at her request, he would not be prosecuted. In response to her request, the Director issued a set of *Guidelines for Prosecutors* in cases relating to assisted suicide. The *Guidelines* did not change the law, but they did ask the prosecutor to consider whether it had been the 'voluntary, clear and settled decision' of the deceased to die and whether the person assisting in the suicide had been 'wholly motivated by compassion'.[5] If these two conditions applied, a prosecution would be unlikely.[6]

After the publication of the *Guidelines*, Debbie Purdy said that she had been 'given her life back', because she now felt that she had the option of committing suicide with her husband's help at some point in the future, without fearing that he would be prosecuted.[7]

Five years later, as we have seen, she spoke of not wanting her life to be 'like this', bedridden and in great pain. For reasons that she did not make clear, she decided to starve herself to death.

The *Guidelines* do not provide a definitive legal ruling on the question of whether assisted suicide should be lawful. All they say is that it depends on the circumstances and the motivation of the individual, and, in so doing, they reflect the prevalent attitude in society today. Assisted suicide is still a crime in the UK, but in many cases those who 'assist' will not be prosecuted.

The Opinion of Doctors

Not surprisingly the question of the ethical acceptability of assisted suicide and euthanasia has been hotly debated within the medical community in recent years. One medical practitioner I spoke to gave his opinion bluntly, saying, 'I did not become a doctor in order to kill my patients.'

At its conference in 2006, the British Medical Association (BMA) voted against assisted death, stating that improvements to palliative care now allowed patients to 'die with dignity'.[8] (Subsequent debates have maintained this position.) The vote brought the BMA into line with a number of other British medical associations, such as the Royal College of General Practitioners and the Royal College of Physicians.[9] Thus, for the time being at least, a majority of British doctors are against assisted suicide.

Patients who are Unable to Make Decisions

So far we have looked at situations where the patient is conscious and able to ask for help to die. However, what happens if the patient is in a long-term unconscious state? Who then makes the decision about continuing life support?

In 1993 the relatives and doctor of a young man called Tony Bland were faced with precisely such a decision. Tony Bland had been crushed against a metal fence after a crowd got out of control at the Hillsborough Football Stadium in Sheffield in 1989. As a result, he suffered brain damage from oxygen starvation, which left him in a PVS state. He could breathe and digest tube-fed food, but there was no evidence that he was conscious or able to respond to his environment in any way.

After three years, his family and medical team applied to the High Court for permission to discontinue feeding and the case eventually went to the House of Lords. The central issue in this case was whether it would be in the best interest of the patient to continue feeding him. The Law Lords decided that, as Tony Bland was not aware of his surroundings and as there was no realistic chance of an improvement in his condition, the treatment that was keeping him alive did not bring him any medical or other benefit.[10] On this basis, artificial feeding was withdrawn and he died some days later.

   To some people this seemed a common-sense decision, but others have argued that this was the point at which British courts ceased to respect the sanctity of human life.[11] It was certainly the first time the courts had accepted as lawful an action whose only purpose was to kill an innocent person.[12]

The Mental Capacity Act

The judgement in the Tony Bland case was a one-off decision. In 2005 a comprehensive new act was introduced, called the *Mental Capacity Act*, whose purpose is to give legal protection to people who lack the capacity to make decisions, for instance, about medical treatment. It stipulates that any decision about life-sustaining treatment for people in this situation 'must not be motivated by a desire to bring about [their] death.'[13] Nevertheless, the act appears to permit the withdrawal of such treatment, if that is considered to be in the patient's best interest.[14] *Treatment* is the key word here, because it is not at all clear whether this is meant to include the provision of food and water. If *treatment* does include these, then withdrawing them could be lawful, according to this Act.

   This interpretation seems to be supported by the information provided on a 2014 NHS public website, which states that, if, after twelve months, there seems to be no hope of recovery for a patient, a court order may be sought to withdraw treatment. If the court agrees, *nutrition* can be withdrawn and 'the person will die peacefully within a few days or weeks.'[15]

In my view, withdrawal of *nutrition*, that is, food, cannot be described as anything other than euthanasia, but the procedure is presented as a compassionate chance for the patient to 'die peacefully', rather than being kept alive with an insufficient *quality of life.*

The NHS recommendation about discontinuing feeding is disturbing, particularly in the light of some recent research into the brain activity of PVS patients. The research, which is being carried out in Cambridge and Liège in Belgium, suggests that PVS patients may be aware of their surroundings, although they are unable to respond to them by external means. The research used MRI scans to detect brain activity in PVS patients and to compare these with the reaction of healthy people acting as controls. As a way of saying 'yes' or 'no' to a question, the doctors asked the patients to imagine, say, playing tennis for 'yes' and moving round their homes for 'no'.

It was known that, in healthy people, these two activities always engage different parts of the brain. Significantly, the PVS patients who responded all activated the same parts of the brain as the healthy controls.[16] The work is still in its early stages, and only a few PVS patients were able to respond, but it does at least suggest caution in relation to decisions about the lives of patients who appear to be unable to react to their surroundings.

US

Because the US consists of many semi-independent states, it is necessary to distinguish between federal laws, applying to all states, and individual state law, applying only in a particular state. In June 1997 the US Supreme Court ruled that citizens do not have a constitutional right to assisted suicide. It therefore fell to individual states to grant or withhold this right. Some states allowed the right, most did not.

The state of Oregon was the first to legalise assisted suicide in October 1997. Its 'Death with Dignity' Act made it legal for patients with less than six months to live to request a prescription for a lethal dose of medication.[17] Since then, assisted suicide has been legalised only in another four of the fifty American states, so the majority of legislators clearly believe that it is not in the interest of a dying person to be helped to take their own life.[18] This is also borne out by the fact that, of the 90,000 people who died in the state of Oregon during the first three years that the act was in force, less than a hundred chose to be helped to die.[19]

Patients who are Unable to Make Decisions

In most American states people have the right to make a living will containing advance decisions about their medical treatment, in case they become unable to do so in the future. These provisions are similar to those of the *Mental Capacity Act* in Britain. In practice, therefore, all Americans have the right to refuse treatment that would prolong their lives in certain specified circumstances.

However, when a patient is not conscious and there is no living will, decisions are often made through the courts, on a case by case basis. The result can be a series of protracted legal battles, as cases are referred from lower to higher courts and repeated appeals are made. This was true particularly in the case of Terri Schiavo, which dragged on for seven years.

In 1990 this lady suffered a cardiac arrest, which left her brain-damaged and unconscious. After a number of failed attempts to bring her to consciousness, the doctors declared that Mrs Schiavo was in a PVS state. When she had been like this for eight years, her husband applied for a court order from the state of Florida where they lived, to have her feeding tube removed. Her parents opposed the application, arguing that their daughter was in fact conscious. There followed seven years of legal battles which turned on whether or not Mrs Schiavo would have wanted to continue living in her present state and what action was therefore in her *best interest*. In 2005 the case went to the US Federal Court, which ordered the removal of Mrs Schiavo's feeding tube, after which she died.[20]

As in the case of Tony Bland, the decision to discontinue feeding was made on the basis of whether or not the patient would have wanted to live in her present condition. It certainly seems unimaginable that anyone would choose to be in a PVS state, but that is not the same as asking to be killed, should one ever fall into such a state.

Here, as in every case of this kind, it is a matter of who decides whether a person lives or dies. Over the last forty years, this question has made itself felt with increasing force in relation to developments in the Netherlands, where euthanasia legislation is applied more and more widely, sometimes without the patient's consent.

The Netherlands

In 2013 a young Dutch woman, who had a degenerative disease, chose to end her life through euthanasia while she was still reasonably healthy rather than suffer the pain of the later stages of the disease.

After consulting her GP, she was accepted for euthanasia, after which she decided to have a documentary made of her lasts days. The film ended with the party for her twenty sixth birthday, at which she danced and sang and drank with her friends. The next day she died after being given a lethal injection of barbiturates. The documentary was shown on Dutch state television and viewed by large numbers of people.[21]

Because Holland has gone further than any other country in the practice of euthanasia, we will consider developments in that country in some detail.

Euthanasia Legislation in the Netherlands

Euthanasia had already been widely practised and tolerated in the Netherlands for several decades before it was finally made legal in 2002. The semi-official approval for the practice before that date can be seen from the fact that a joint commission of the Dutch government and the Royal Dutch Medical Association (KNMG) published guidelines for it in 1982.[22] These specified that a request for euthanasia must be given of the patient's free will, that it must be well-considered and lasting, that there must be unacceptable suffering; in addition, two doctors must evaluate each case.

Surprisingly, the commission also recommended that non-voluntary euthanasia should be decriminalised, if it was carried out in the context of 'careful medical practice'; the term was not defined and contradicts the requirement that patients should only be euthanised of their own free will.

Since legalisation there has been a rise from less than 2000 euthanasia deaths in 2003 to over 4000 in 2012, so reported euthanasia deaths have more than doubled in this decade.[23] The rise can be accounted for partly by an increase in demand and partly by an ever-widening interpretation of the rules under which euthanasia may be performed.

In 2011 the KNMG drafted new guidelines, according to which social factors, such as loneliness and low income, combined with non-terminal diseases, might qualify a patient for euthanasia.[24] The fact that it is virtually impossible to provide objective criteria for what is 'unbearable', means that many euthanasia decisions are made on a basis of wholly or partly subjective criteria. In the end, the decision depends on whether the patient wants to live or not.

Euthanasia of Newborns

One group which is certainly unable to make a decision about their own lives is seriously ill newborns. These are not covered by the Dutch euthanasia law, but in cases where the outlook is poor and the parents give their consent, any doctor who agrees to end the child's life is unlikely to be prosecuted. According to a recent study, between 1997 and 2005, there were only twenty-two reported cases, none of which led to prosecution.[25] Nevertheless these infants were killed solely because they were seriously ill and in pain, so that their lives were not thought worth living.

There is a parallel here with the destruction of so-called defective embryos and the abortion of handicapped and sick foetuses. Here, too, it is assumed that the human being who is killed would not have wanted to live, if he or she could have expressed an opinion. The motivation for these killings is often compassionate, but other reasons, such as the desire for a good life or even a convenient life, can also influence the decision.

Euthanasia as a Life-Style Choice

The link between euthanasia and the search for a good life can be seen in a recent Dutch citizens' proposal, called 'Out of Free Will'. The proposal calls for access to euthanasia for any person over seventy who feels that his or her life is 'complete' and wishes to end it at a moment of their choosing. One of the leaders of the movement, a feminist and former minister, has argued that she felt she had a right to choose her time of death as 'a natural extension of her lifelong battle for emancipation.'[26] Her comments are significant, because the whole euthanasia movement is focused on being in charge not only of one's life, but also of one's death.

However, the choice of the moment of death can easily be taken from a sick person by somebody else, as is already beginning to happen in the Netherlands.

Defending My Life

The fear of misuse of the euthanasia legislation has led to the formation of the *Dutch Patients' Association*, a disability rights organisation which has produced wallet-sized cards stating that, if the signatory is admitted to a hospital 'no treatment be administered with the intention to terminate life.'[27] It is doubly significant that this card was introduced in 1990, some ten years before euthanasia was made legal in Holland, but during a period when euthanasia, though illegal, was nevertheless tolerated. For some, often the weakest and those least able to make their wishes known, the legal right to choose assisted dying or euthanasia has brought with it the fear that others will make that choice on their behalf, against their will.

Public Opinion about Assisted Dying

In spite of the ominous developments in the Netherlands, majority public opinion in countries where assisted suicide and euthanasia are illegal continues to support these practices, at least for some patients. For instance, at the time of writing, there is yet another bill before Parliament to legalise assisted dying in the UK.

UK

A survey of public attitudes to assisted suicide and euthanasia over the twenty-year period from 1984 to 2005 showed an overwhelming majority in favour of legalising euthanasia for incurable patients in great pain who wished to die.[28]

The level of interest in these topics can also be seen from the unprecedented number of responses to the consultation before the publication of the *Guidelines for Public Prosecutors* that was mentioned earlier. Some 5,000 individuals from all walks of life took part, including health care professionals and those representing religious groups.[29]

Help to die means asking someone else to make it possible for the patient to die. Often this person is the doctor, but the beliefs and attitudes of doctors tend to be overlooked. It is not surprising that a recent survey of UK doctors revealed that a majority was opposed both to assisted suicide and euthanasia as a matter of principle.[30] Most doctors want to save lives, not destroy them. Also, many doctors still swear the Hippocratic oath, which includes the promise that 'I will not give poison to anyone though asked to do so, nor will I suggest such a plan.'[31]

It is revealing that some of the doctors in the UK survey suggested that, if assisted dying was legalised, those who assisted should not be doctors, but belong to a separate profession, set up with this specific task in mind. This sinister proposal reveals with all possible clarity that, if patients are going to be killed, few doctors want to do it.

US

In the US public support for assisted suicide has varied over the last twenty years, but a majority of those surveyed have been in favour throughout the period.[32] Support for access to euthanasia for incurably ill patients has steadily increased, with about two thirds of respondents in favour in 2013.[33]

On the other hand, a recent poll of medical practitioners has shown that only a small majority, just over half, were in favour of euthanasia for the terminally ill.[34] As in the UK, a significant proportion of doctors do not want to take the lives of their patients.

The Netherlands

There are not many polls of the general public in Holland, but those that exist reveal a majority in favour of euthanasia in some form. According to a poll taken in 2002, the year in which euthanasia was legalised, about two thirds of those surveyed were in favour of giving the elderly the right to die, while three quarters supported the controlled distribution of 'suicide pills' to those who felt that their lives were 'completed'.[35]

A survey of doctors in 2011 revealed that a large majority felt under increasing pressure to carry out euthanasia. Regardless of their personal views, most said that they were willing to cooperate with such a request and nearly all felt that it had a place in medicine.[36] If this poll is an accurate reflection of medical opinion in Holland, then Dutch doctors differ significantly from their American and, especially, their British colleagues.

The Slippery Slope: From Right to Die to Duty to Die

One of the arguments against legalising assisted dying is that such a law would inevitably be used to pressurise people into accepting help to die. On the other hand, the main argument in favour is that some seriously ill people who wished to die would be given the means of doing so. In a widely reported article Baroness Warnock, who taught philosophy at Oxford and Cambridge and chaired a number of government committees on medical ethics, has argued that, in some circumstances, sick or dependent people might feel not only a desire to die for their own sake, but a duty to die for the sake of their families and society in general. She compared such a death to 'falling on one's sword', stating that the practice might regain the place of honour it once held in ancient Rome.[37] She argued that there was no reason to believe that the legalisation of assisted dying would lead to people being forced to die, as it had not had any 'disastrous consequences' in the Netherlands, Belgium and Switzerland, where the practice was already legal.

However, as we have seen, in the Netherlands many disabled people now carry cards stating that they do not wish to be euthanised, precisely because they fear that they might be forced to die against their will. It would seem that the duty to die that Lady Warnock describes in such lofty terms could all too easily become imposed rather than chosen.

Palliative Care: Respect for Life till the End of Life

Palliative care is the life-affirming alternative to assisted suicide and euthanasia. The word *palliative* comes from the Latin *pallium*, which means a cloak, so that the person who gives palliative care can be said to wrap a comforting cloak around the suffering person, almost like putting their arms around them.

The purpose of palliative care is to give people in the last stages of terminal illness the best chance of living out their days as fully as possible. It involves care of the whole person, including specialist pain management. This kind of care can be given in a hospice, at home or in a mainstream hospital and although much palliative care is motivated by the Christian faith, there are also hospices run on a secular basis.[38]

Palliative Care: Origin

How did palliative care begin? As so often happens, an imaginative person asked a question that no one else had asked before. In this case, the person was the Swiss-American doctor Elizabeth Kuebler-Ross who met many terminally ill patients through her work. She asked herself the question, 'What does it actually feel like to be dying?' The only way to find out was to talk to, and listen to, her dying patients.

This was how she began her ground-breaking research into death and dying in the late 1950s. She recorded her experiences in her book *On Death and Dying*, which has become a classic on the subject and the basis for much subsequent palliative care. She stressed the need to tell the patients as much of the truth as they could bear at the time, but also the importance of trying to put yourself in their situation. She discovered that what counted most for terminally ill people was a sense that the doctor knew how they felt and, even more importantly, was able to feel with them.[39]

However, it is only possible to feel with another person, if one acknowledges the truth about that person's condition. This is the opposite of seeking to control the patient's situation either through pointless treatment or through euthanasia. In both of these two extreme situations, the doctor is interfering in the life of the dying person, rather than accompanying him or her in truth and compassion.

Although the demand for palliative care has been growing in recent years, it is not associated with the same high-profile campaigning as the demand for assisted suicide and euthanasia.

Palliative Care in the UK, the US and the Netherlands

Palliative care has been recognised as a medical speciality in the UK since 1987, but it is still very much a Cinderella service. In recent years average government support for hospice provision in England has only covered a third of the total cost, the rest coming from charitable giving. In spite of the financial difficulties, the speciality has grown, so that, in 2010, there were about 330 full-time medical personnel working in the field. Even so, this is not enough to keep up with a growing demand.[40]

In a results-oriented culture, the lack of adequate public funding for palliative care is not surprising. Looking after the dying does not achieve measurable results in the same way as, for instance, an increase in the number of patients who survive many years after a cancer operation.

The increase in demand for hospice care has also made itself felt in the US, where the majority of hospice patients fund their treatment via a Government-funded medical service.[41] During the quarter century from 1985 to 2009, the number of hospices in the US trebled, while the number of patients treated in hospices rose about fifteen-fold from one hundred thousand in 1984 to about one and a half million in 2009. In that year almost half of all deaths in the US occurred under the care of a hospice pro-gramme, either in a hospice or in the patient's home. It appears that provision of this kind of service is better in the US than in the UK.

As assisted dying is more widely available in the Neth-erlands than in most other countries and as many Dutch people see this as the best way to approach the last stages of life, it is not surprising that hospice care is not well developed in that country. Thus, in the mid-1990s there were only two hospice programmes, providing very limited services.[42] By the year 2000, the number of people dying in hospices was negligible compared with deaths at home, in hospitals and in nursing homes.[43] Nevertheless, the fact that palliative care exists at all in the Netherlands, shows that assisted suicide and euthanasia are not the only responses to terminal illness in that country.

Christian Attitudes to the End of Life

Palliative care is the only approach to the end of life that treats it as a gift rather than a possession that can be disposed of at will. This agrees with the teaching of both the Old and the New Testaments, which make it clear that God is the sole giver of human life. The commandment, 'You shall not kill', means that no one has the right to kill an innocent human being, including oneself. That does not mean that believers do not at times wish they were dead, but wishing one was dead is not the same as deciding to kill oneself or asking for euthanasia.

Elijah in the Desert

The Old Testament has a vivid description of the feelings of a man who no longer wishes to live. The ninth century prophet Elijah was pursued by the followers of the cruel Queen Jezebel, who had slaughtered all the other prophets of the kingdom of Israel. The account of his flight into the desert in near-despair at the Queen's plans to have him killed too, shows him, 'sitting under a furze bush [wishing] he were dead;' but, instead of giving in to despair, he turns to God in trust, saying, 'I have had enough. Take my life; I am no better than my ancestors.'[44] Elijah acknowledges that only God can give and take life; at the same time he tells the Lord, 'This is how I feel. I can see no way out.'

He then lies down, expecting to die, but God answers his prayer, not with death, but with the means to carry on. The angel of the Lord wakes him and says, 'Get up and eat'; and there, before him, was a simple meal of a scone and water. Encouraged, Elijah eats and drinks and then tries to go back to sleep. He is still not convinced that he can continue as a prophet.

The angel then touches him again and tells him to eat and drink some more, otherwise he will not be able to survive the long journey to Mount Horeb where God will reveal himself.[45] Elijah walks for forty days and forty nights to reach the mountain, only to be told that he must go back the way he came to proclaim the Lord's message to his rebellious people. No longer in despair, because he trusts completely in God, Elijah accepts his hard task.

Christ on the Cross

Christ himself felt the full force of the temptation to despair that can accompany extreme suffering. Nailed to the Cross he felt utterly alone, so that he cried out,

> My God, my God, why have you forsaken me?

This could sound as if he thought God the Father had really abandoned him. However, it is the first line of a psalm which continues with expressions of trust in God,

> In you our fathers put their trust;
> they trusted and you set them free ...
> I will tell of your name to my brethren
> and praise you where they are assembled.[46]

With this psalm, Christ was really saying, 'I feel abandoned, but nevertheless, I trust in you, my God, and I obey your will for me.' He meant the suffering of remaining on the Cross, even though, as Son of God, he had the power to end it.

This is important, because most of us will feel the same sense of abandonment at some point in our lives. In such a situation, the only thing to do is to remember that, in spite of how he felt, Christ trusted and accepted the will of God. Because of this, we, too, can accept in trust.

When I myself was in severe pain for which there did not seem to be a cure, the thought that Christ stayed on the Cross, although he had the power to come down, was the one thing that helped me.

Church Teaching

In one of his official documents, Pope St John Paul II said that, in contemporary society, life is often seen as worthwhile only when it is accompanied by happiness and physical well-being, so that suffering must be avoided at all costs.[47] In view of the medical skills available now, he stated that people today can be strongly tempted to 'take control of death and bring it about before its time.' According to the Pope, those who have this attitude also tend to see the growing number of elderly and disabled people as an intolerable burden.[48]

As a result, more and more people turn to euthanasia as a means of achieving a good life in the sense of a life free from pain and disability and, for those who look after the sick, a life free from the burden of caring.

However, Pope John Paul did not call for disproportionate measures to preserve life. He made it clear that there is a difference between euthanasia and the acknowledgement that further treatment is pointless.[49] Christ, too, lived through those last moments of life, when it is clear that death is approaching. Acknowledging what was about to happen, he therefore turned to his Father and said,

Father, into your hands I commit my spirit.[50]

Abigail's Story

Acceptance of life as a gift stands in direct opposition to attempts to control life and manage death. This principle is best illustrated through the story of a young woman who, while almost totally paralysed, gave a moving witness to her belief that the value of human life does not depend on our ability to do things, but rather on our God-given humanity.

Abigail Witchalls, a young mother expecting her second child, was out for a walk with her toddler son, when she was attacked by a mentally disturbed man. He stabbed her in the neck, severing much of her spinal cord, and then fled, leaving her for dead. When she was brought into hospital, almost totally paralysed, the doctors thought it might be better simply to leave her to die. Yet, inside her paralysed body, Abigail was very much alive. What follows is based on an article in which her mother, Sheila Hollins, described how the attack had affected her daughter and the whole family.

During the first few weeks, Abigail could only communicate by blinking. Nevertheless, through this slender means of communication, she was able to dictate this short poem to a relative, letter by letter,

> Still silent body
> But within my spirit sings
> Dancing in love-light.[51]

Abigail, who was from a Catholic family, gradually regained the power of speech and some limited movement and was able to return home and to give birth to a healthy baby boy.

Many people would have agreed with the doctors that, for someone in her condition, it would have been better if she, and her baby, had been allowed to die. Her mother, who is a professor of psychiatry, spoke honestly about the difficulty for the whole family of coming to terms with what had happened, but also of their continued hope for further improvement. She said that she thought Abigail's paralysis may have called all the family 'to greater strength and to a different path in life'.[52]

The title of the article, 'Blessings in Abundance', showed that the family, and above all Abigail herself, were convinced that life could indeed be good, even and, in a sense, especially, in the difficult circumstances they now faced.

This attitude contrasts sharply with that of Debbie Purdy, who said she did not want her life to be 'like this' and therefore committed suicide. Abigail accepted her life, even though she could only communicate her thoughts by blinking.

Conclusion: Assisted Suicide and Euthanasia

In today's society there is a growing demand for control of every aspect of human life, including the moment of death. As a consequence more and more people call for a right to death comparable to the right to life contained in the *Declaration of Human Rights*. In these circumstances every one of us is faced with the question, 'Who is in charge of life, God or man?'

If we become convinced, as Adam and Eve did, that man can be in charge and we act on that assumption, then quality control creeps in and every life may be in danger. This development has not happened as a sudden seismic shift, but rather by degrees, so that it is more difficult to detect and therefore more dangerous.

If we press for a right to death, however compassionate our motives, we may have unleashed a threat that we could not have foreseen, but that some elderly patients are now beginning to fear.

On the other hand, if we accept life as a gift from God which only God has the right to take back, then we will respect everyone, however frail or handicapped. We will then affirm the right to life that most of us have taken for granted for so long and that we tamper with at our peril.

Overall Summary

- In our times people tend to be valued for their abilities rather than their humanity.
- Assisted suicide and euthanasia have become growing threats to the lives of the seriously handicapped and sick.
- Euthanasia is often presented as an act of compassion, intended to put an end to suffering.
- Palliative care eases suffering while respecting life.
- Christians believe that life is a gift from God which no one has the right to destroy.
- Respect for life at its end does not imply the disproportionate use of medical procedures.
- The legalisation of assisted dying is based mainly on a popular demand.
- Ordinary people can reduce the incidence of assisted suicide and euthanasia by deciding not to use them.

Those who end human life for the sake of a good life do not always do so in a medical context. Individuals who are prepared to kill in order to achieve a particular goal are called terrorists and our next chapter is concerned with the threat to human life that they present in today's world.

Notes

1   As reported *in* T*he Guardian*, 29 December 2014.

2   Leading article *in The Times*, 5 January 2012. The report of the commission on assisted dying chaired by Lord Falconer, was reported in the same issue of *The Times*.

3   Patients' Rights Council, 'Background about Euthanasia in the Netherlands', http://www.patientsrightscouncil.org/site/holland-background/ (11 October 2011).

4   Report in *The Guardian*, 20 October 2006.

5   'Policy for Prosecutors in Respect of Cases of Encouraging or Assisting Suicide', February 2010, nos. 45.1–2. http://www.cps.gov.uk/publications/prosecution/assisted_suicide_policy.html (23 August 2010).

6   As reported in *The Times* 25 February 2010.

7   As reported in *The Times* 26 February 2010.

8   *Press Association Report*, 29 June 2006.

9   Other associations taking this stance are; the Association of Palliative Medicine, the Royal College of Psychiatrists and the Royal College of Nurses. Julian Hughes, 'Killing Mrs Nobody', *in The Tablet* 15 July 2006.

10 J. Wyatt *Matters of Life and Death*, (Leicester:Intervarsity Press, 1998), p. 17, including a quotation from the House of Lords Judgement.

11 P. Singer, *Rethinking Life and Death*, (Oxford:Oxford University Press, 1995), p. 68. as quoted by J. Wyatt, John Wyatt *Matters of Life and Death*, (Leicester:Intervarsity Press, 1998), p. 17.

12 Wyatt *Matters of Life and Death*, p. 17.

13 *Mental Capacity Act* s.4(5), http://www.opsi.gov.uk/acts/acts2005/20050009.htm (2 April 2007).

14 *Mental Capacity Act* s.4(5–10), http://www.opsi.gov.uk/acts/acts2005/20050009.htm (2 April 2007).

15 NHS choices, Vegetative State, http://www.nhs.uk/conditions/Vegetative-state/Pages/Introduction.aspx (28 October 2011).

16 As reported *in The Times* 4 February 2010, citing *the New England Journal of Medicine*. M.M. Monti and other, 'Wilful modulation of brain activity in disorders of consciousness', *in The New England Journal of Medicine*, vol. 362/7,pp. 579–89.

17 Oregon State website oregon.gov.

18   'Physician Assisted Suicide', Ontario Consultants on Religious Tolerance, http://www.religioustolerance.org/euth_us3.htm (16 December 2010).

19   *Aging in the Know*, 'Ethical and Legal Issues', p. 15. http://www.healthinaging.org/agingintheknow/chapters_ch_trial.asp?ch=4 (4 October 2011).

20   See 'the Terri Schiavo case', Wikipedia article with legal references.   http://en.wikipedia.org/wikli/Terri_Schiavo_case   (3 October 2011).

21   https://www.lifesitenews.com/news/film-depicting-euthanasia-of-26-year-old-dutch-woman-draws-70000-viewers (29 May 2015).

22   'Guidelines for Euthanasia' (KNMG), tr. W. Lagerwey, *in Issues Law Med.* 1988, No. 3, pp. 429–437.

23   Figures from Alex Schadenberg, report *on LifeSiteNews.com*, 16 June 2010, http://www.lifesitenews.com/home/print_article /news/2205/ (6 October 2011), www.patientsrightscouncil.org /site/holland / quoting from Dutch Central Bureau of Statistics andhttp://alexschadenberg.blogspot.co.uk/2013/09/netherlands-euthanasia-report-indicates.html (12 December 2012).

24   *Radio Netherlands Worldwide*, print version 8 September 2011, http://www.rnw.nl/english/print/480429 (5 October 2011).

25   A.A Verhagen and others, 'Deliberate termination of life in newborns in the Netherlands; review of all 22 reported cases between 1997 and 2004'. *Ned Tijdschr. Geneeskd* Vol. 149, no. 37, pp. 2067–9. PMID 16184950.

26   As reported *in Radio Netherlands Worldwide*, February 2010, http://www.rnw.nl/english/article/right-die-elderly-back-centre-dutch-debate (5 October 2011).

27   Patients' Rights Council, 'Background about Euthanasia in the Netherlands', http://www.patientsrightscouncil.org/site/holland-background/ (11 October 2011).

28   E. Clery, S. McLean and M. Phillips, 'Quickening death: the euthanasia debate', *in British Social Attitudes*, 23rd Report, Ed. Alison Park et al. (London:SAGE Publications Ltd, 2007), p. 48f., Table 2.5.

29   As reported in *The Times*, 26 February 2010.

30   C. Seale, 'Legalisation of euthanasia or physician-assisted suicide: survey of doctors' attitudes' in *Palliative Medicine* vol. 23 (2009), pp. 207–212. http://www.eapcnet.eu/LinkClick.aspx?fileticket=

2EQi4VJBHnk%3D&tabid=38 (23 December 2013).

[31]   Wyatt,*Matters of Life and Death*, p. 216.

[32]   Gallup Polls, May 2013, http://www.gallup.com/poll/162815/ support-euthanasia-hinges-described.aspx (19 December 2013).

[33]   Gallup Polls, May 2013, http://www.gallup.com/poll/162815/ support-euthanasia-hinges-described.aspx (19 December 2013).

[34]   'Euthanasia Statistics' http://www.statisticbrain.com/euthanasia-statistics/ based on polls by Gallup, Angelfire and Nightingale Alliance. (19 December 2013).

[35]   *Radio Netherlands Worldwide*, FAQ 'Euthanasia in the Netherlands', 2009, http://www.rnw.nl/english/article/faq-%E2%80%93-euthanasia-netherlands (20 December 2013).

[36]   http://www.freerepublic.com/focus/f-news/2756010/posts quoting LifeSiteNews (20 December 2013).

[37]   *Omsorg* (Care), 4/2008, pp.3–5.

[38]   For example, East Anglia Children's Hospices seeks to give spiritual support, but not necessarily on a religious basis. http://www.each.org.uk/index.php?option=com_content&task= view&id=170&Itemid=192 (22 November 2007).and St. Joseph's Hospice, London, which is open to people of any religion or none, was founded by Roman Catholic Sisters of Charity and its trustees all belong this order. http://www.stjh.org.uk/who_we_are/ stjosephshistory.html and http://www.stjh.org.uk/who_we_are/ whoiswho.html (4 August 2008).

[39]   E. Kuebler-Ross *On Death and Dying*, (1970). Reprint (London: Routledge, 2001), p. 33.

[40]   Joint Royal College of Physicians Training Board, 'Palliative Medicine', Introduction, http://www.jrcptb.org.uk/specialities/ ST3-SpR/Pages/Palliative-Medicine.aspx (16 September 2011).

[41]   'Hospice Care Statistics', http://www.yalemedicalgroup.org/stw/ Page.asp?PageID=STW023255 , Yale School of Medicine 2011, (16 September 2011).

[42]   'Background about Euthanasia in the Netherlands', Patients Rights Council, 2011, http://www.patientsrightscouncil.org/site/ holland-background/ (21 September 2011), citing *Euthanasia: Report of the Working Party to Review the British Medical Association's Guidance on Euthanasia*, British Medical Association, 5 May, 1988, no. 195, p. 49 and R. L. Marker, *Deadly Compassion – The Death of Ann Humphry and the Truth about Euthanasia* , (New York: William Morrow, 1993), p. 157.

[43]   'Better Palliative Care for Older People', WHO Report 2004, p. 21, http://www.euro.who.int/_data/assets/pdf_file/0009/98235/E82933.pdf (21 September 2011)

[44]   1 K 19:4.

[45]   1 K 19:6–8. Mount Horeb is thought to have been in the Southern part of the Sinai Peninsula, but its exact location is uncertain. See *The New Jerusalem Bible*, Standard Edition, (London:Darton, Longman & Todd, 1985), note b for Ex 19:2.

[46]   Ps 21(22) 5,21.

[47]   Pope John Paul II, *Evangelium Vitae*, 64. Italics in the original.

[48]   *Ibid.*

[49]   *Ibid*, 65.

[50]   Lk 23:46.

[51]   Quoted in S. Hollins, 'Blessings in Abundance', *The Tablet* 17/24 December 2005.

[52]   *Ibid.*

5 THREATS TO HUMAN LIFE: TERRORISM

HARDLY A DAY goes by without news reports of yet more terrorist attacks somewhere in the world. Often there are also reports of pressure groups seeking to impose their views by milder forms of violence, such as disrupting an event to gain publicity for their cause.

I once talked to a fellow student about a play she had been to, or rather, a play she had demonstrated at. She said that she and a group of others had got up during the performance and shouted and waved banners in support of their cause. When I said that I thought it was inconsiderate both to the actors and the audience to do such a thing, she replied that there were so few opportunities to express your views in today's society that it was necessary to use every means possible, even if it upset some people. Clearly, she had lost faith in democratic means of convincing others of her beliefs and in this she is not alone.

At least the demonstration she was involved with did not hurt anyone physically, but it did spoil the evening for a lot of people. However, what if her group had thrown bombs rather than waved banners? The group would still have been trying to further a particular aim, but now with such extreme means that they killed people in the process.

At this point, it is natural to ask what level of violence is acceptable in a demonstration? Personally, I do not think force of any kind has a place, because it is a means of forcing other people to act in a particular way. Therefore

I would not condone even comparatively mild forms, such as disrupting a play.

Banner-waving and bomb-throwing represent the two extremes on a sliding scale with direct action at one end and terrorism at the other. For our purposes, the most important aspect of terrorism is the threat it presents to human life for the sake of a perceived good life; it therefore belongs with the other threats treated in this book.

The motivation for both terrorism and direct action is often similar in that those who use these methods seek to achieve a goal by force rather than persuasion. Terrorists systematically use violence and intimidation to achieve a goal, whereas people engaged in direct action typically use sit-downs or sabotage to achieve their aims. It must be added that terrorism exists only on the margins of society, while direct action has rather wider support. Nevertheless, in order to understand the mind-set that can lead to terrorism, it is necessary to begin by looking at direct action and its causes first.

Direct Action as a First Step towards Terrorism

Direct action is often the result of disillusionment with the democratic process. A recent action by the British MP Caroline Lucas provides a telling example of this. In order to prevent fracking (splitting rocks to obtain gas or oil) in a particular location, the former leader of the Green Party sat down in the access road to the proposed site, thereby preventing vehicles from reaching it. She referred to her action as a 'peaceful protest', saying that she was concerned about the impact of fracking on the environment. Through her role in Parliament, she could have tried to persuade her fellow MPs of the rightness of her cause.[1] Instead she used direct action to prevent others from doing something she disagreed with. When even an MP has so little faith in democracy that she resorts to direct action, it is not surprising that many ordinary people no longer take the trouble to vote, but seek other means of achieving their aims.

As a protest against government spending cuts in the UK in 2010, there was a string of direct actions in the country. These varied from demonstrations by public sector workers, to occupation of Vodafone stores in response to the company's large tax break, to student marches and sit-ins at universities. Demonstrators also damaged property by breaking into Conservative Party campaign headquarters in London.[2]

Damage to property is violence against things, but such violence can at times lead to violence against people. This is where the boundaries between direct action and terrorism become blurred and where human life can be at risk. Although it is true that few people who take part in direct action intend to engage in terrorism, the use of such action is often a means of getting other people to behave in a particular way through force rather than genuine persuasion. The step into terrorism can then be a short one.

At the G8 Summit in 2007 some of the protesters undoubtedly took this short step. The summits, which have regularly been targets for environmental and political protests, provide a forum for the most powerful nations of the world to discuss important issues of the day, such as climate change. On this occasion, the protesters sought to prevent delegates from arriving at the venue by blocking the roads leading from the nearest airport. When this failed, some of them began to burn cars, smash shop fronts and attack members of the police. Once the violence had reached this extreme, even some of the organisers described it as totally unjustifiable.[3]

Some of the most violent forms of direct action in recent years have been aimed not at organisations or international gatherings, but at individuals working for particular firms. For example, in order to prevent medical experimentation on live animals by firms such as *Huntingdon Life Science*, protesters have not contented themselves with gathering outside the firm's headquarters, but have also demonstrated outside the homes of the firm's employees. The intimidation did not stop there, because some demonstrators went on to attack the homes and, in some cases, the employees themselves.

When the managing director of the firm arrived home from work one day, he was attacked with pickaxe handles and so badly beaten that he needed hospital treatment. A businessman linked to the firm was also beaten up and left unconscious by his burning barn, which the attackers had set alight. Fortunately he regained consciousness, so that he was able to avoid being burnt to death. In these cases and others like them, the protesters had clearly moved from demonstrating to violence and intimidation.[4]

Why Direct Action?

It is difficult to get precise figures for how frequently direct action takes place, but it does seem to be happening more and more frequently in recent times. Why do people resort to this form of action? In my view, there are two main reasons, a disillusionment with the democratic process and a desire for instant results.

One of the most important aspects of democracy is the opportunity to vote in free elections. The number of people who choose to do so is therefore a clear indicator of how important democracy is to them. For instance, in the general elections in the UK there has been a dramatic drop in voting, from over 80% in 1950 to about 60% in 2001.[5] In spite of a slight recovery since then, there is still a significant lack of interest in using the vote in contemporary Britain.

In the US, the decline in interest can best be illustrated from the voter turnout in presidential elections. In 1960 the turnout was well over 60%, whereas in 2008 it dropped to only about 55%. The drop in voter numbers is not as great as in the UK, but, nevertheless, the lower percentage is striking, as 2008 was the year in which President Obama was elected to the White House.[6] If almost half the electorate could not be bothered to vote, even in the year in which the first black candidate had a realistic chance of being returned, then faith in the democratic process is surely in decline.

The second reason for the increase in direct action is the tendency today to seek instant gratification in every area of life. For instance, advertising plays into the hands of this development by offering instant access to consumer goods. Why wait for the sofa, tablet or car if I can get them now? So, in the political arena, why wait for change through the ballot box and persuasion, if I can get it now, by force? This is where direct action can easily become terrorism.

Terrorism

Like his close cousin, the extreme direct activist, the terrorist has lost faith in the democratic process, or perhaps never had it. The terrorist does not believe in persuasion or negotiation, but only in what he thinks will achieve what he wants. Terrorism is used for many different purposes, for instance to prevent experiments on animals or as part of anti-abortion campaigns, but today it is employed largely to achieve political and religious aims and we will therefore focus on some significant examples from these two areas. Before going any further, is important to stress that, whenever a group seeks to achieve a goal through terrorism, there is usually also an organisation aiming at the same goal through peaceful means.

Political Terrorism

The fight of militant Zionists to establish a Jewish state after the Second World War provides a good example of politically motivated terrorism. In the years leading up to the establishment of the State of Israel, Zionists carried out terrorist acts to achieve their nation state by force. The best-known such act was the bombing in 1946 of the *King David Hotel* in Jerusalem, which was the civilian and military headquarters of the British forces in Palestine. Over eighty people were killed, including British, Arabs and Jews who worked in the building.

The attack was carried out by an organisation called *Irgun*, led by Menachem Begin, who went on to become Prime Minister of Israel. Sadly, the terrorist methods he had used in order to establish a Jewish homeland meant that his organisation had begun to mete out the same brutal treatment to others that the Jewish people had been subjected to in so many countries over the centuries and especially during the Second World War in Nazi Germany.

Later in life, Begin sought to justify this and other terrorist acts in his book *The Revolt: The Story of Irgun*. He spoke of his organisation beginning to 'fight instead of to plead', which are words that reverberate through all terrorist action.[7]

Irgun was not the only Jewish organisation fighting for a homeland. Mainstream Zionism, represented by *Haganah*, aimed to practise a policy of restraint in pursuit of the same aim.[8]

Politico-Religious Terrorism

Closer to our own times, the terrorist attacks on the US in September 2001 and on the UK in July 2005 have become emblems of the disregard for human life that characterises all terrorism.

The 9/11 attacks on the *World Trade Center* in New York and other American targets were motivated by a mixture of political and fundamentalist religious aims. In 1998 Osama bin Laden, the extremist Muslim leader, issued a fatwa (religious decree) listing US actions which, in his view, were crimes and sins, for which the country ought to be punished. These included US military occupation of the Arabian Peninsula, US aggression against the Iraqi people and US support for Israel.[9] The punishment consisted of four co-ordinated attacks which were intended to force the US government to pull out of the Middle East.[10] In so doing, Bin Laden's followers killed almost 3,000 people most of whom had nothing to do with US policy in the Middle East. This was terrorism almost as a military action, which caused death and destruction on an unprecedented scale without achieving the change in US policy that had been its aim.

Like the 9/11 attacks in the US, the 7/7 attacks in London appeared to be co-ordinated, so that they had some of the features of a military attack. However, unlike the 9/11 attacks, they did not seem to have an immediate political goal in view. According to one commentator, the attacks, which targeted the underground and bus network of the capital, were aimed at forcing the British to accept Islam as their religion and to set up an Islamic state, both of which could only be regarded as very long-term aims.[11] It seems highly likely that the more immediate goal was to kill as many non-Muslims as possible, as these were supposed to be enemies of Islam. The terrorists succeeded in killing fifty-six people, including themselves, as well as injuring hundreds of others. However, if their long-term goals were to convert people to Islam, they could hardly have chosen a worse means of persuasion.

The behaviour of such extremists is not accepted by mainstream Islam. On the very day of the attacks in London, *Churches Together in Britain and Ireland* and *The Muslim Council of Britain* issued a joint statement condemning the attacks. They went on to say that the scriptures and traditions of both the Muslim and Christian religions reject violence.[12] Thus its use by an extremist religious faction had united mainstream Christians and Muslims in a joint condemnation of terrorism.

Threats from Terrorist Acts Compared with Threats from Embryo Destruction, Abortion and Assisted Dying

Since the 9/11 and 7/7 attacks, there have been many others in which large numbers of people have been killed. As I write, some forty people, most of them British, have been gunned down on a beach in Tunisia, apparently in the name of an extremist Islamist organisation.

With so many terrorist attacks all over the world, it can seem as if this is one of the main threats to human life today; however, that is far from being the case. Although different people and organisations define terrorism differently, deaths from such attacks can be counted in tens of thousands, whereas deaths due to embryo destruction and abortion are counted in millions. Even deaths due to assisted suicide and euthanasia are higher than than those from terrorism. Medical threats at the beginning and end of life are therefore the greater dangers to human life today.

During the forty years from 1969 to 2009 one report of terrorism deaths worldwide came to about 60,000, a higher number than some other reports.[13] Even if we accept this figure, embryo and abortion deaths amount to much larger numbers. For instance, we know that during the approximately fifteen years between 1991 and 2005, embryo deaths in the UK alone came to over one million. Abortion deaths were also much higher than those caused by terrorism. In the UK, there were over seven million such deaths during the period from 1968 to 2010. In the US there were forty million abortions between 1973 and 2006.

Exact numbers for deaths from assisted suicide and euthanasia are hard to come by, but it seems that there were 3,600 such deaths in the Netherlands during 2009, over twice as many as the 1500 terrorism fatalities worldwide in the same year. Bearing in mind that the worldwide number of assisted deaths must be much higher than the Dutch figure, such deaths, at least in 2009, were considerably higher than deaths from terror attacks. Nevertheless, it is the current threat to the embryo and the unborn child that is so shockingly high in our times.

Both the terrorist attacks and the medical procedures we have considered are based on the belief that the end justifies the means and both involve a judgement about the value of particular human lives. However, there is a an important difference. The terrorist does not care who or what he (or she) destroys in the attack. Those involved in destroying embryos, unborn children or sick people are to a great extent moved by compassion, as they do not want anyone to have to live with a serious illness or disability, or a child they cannot cope with. Unfortunately, this attitude leads to a labelling of certain categories of human beings as disposable and we will come back to this topic in the next chapter. For the moment, let us consider Christian teaching about direct action and terrorism.

The Attitude of Christianity to Direct Action and Terrorism

There are two passages in Scripture that could appear to condone terrorism on the one hand and direct action on the other, so that they require some explanation. The first tells the story of Samson, the Old Testament leader with super-human strength who destroyed the enemies of his people at the cost of his own life. The second is the account of Christ expelling the money-changers from the Temple in the New Testament.

The Old Testament and Terrorism

In the Old Testament there are two apparently conflicting attitudes to the use of violence. One reveals a concept of God as a warrior God who fights for his Chosen People, the other a gradually emerging understanding of God as a suffering God, who does not impose his will by force.

The story of Samson reflects the former idea of God as someone who protects the Israelite armies in battle and who gives individual Jewish leaders the strength to kill their enemies.[14] The setting for this tale is a primitive society, in which the Jews are fighting to stay in possession of the Promised Land.[15]

Samson had left his hair uncut as the outward sign of a life dedicated to the service of God. In return the Lord had granted him super-human strength for the protection of his people, as long as he kept his vow not to cut his hair.

All goes well for Samson, until he falls in love with a lady called Delilah, who is a spy for his enemies, the Philistines. She manages to wheedle his secret out of him, that if his hair is ever cut, he will lose his strength. Needless to say, she finds an opportunity to lull him to sleep and then cuts his hair, so that he loses his strength; the Philistines can now capture him and blind him. As a further humiliation, they chain him and set him to work turning a mill stone. After he has been working like this for a long time, his hair begins to grow again, which means that his strength might be returning.[16]

In the last chapter of Samson's life, God gives him a chance to serve his people and at the same time redeem himself for breaking his vow. When the Philistines take him into their temple to give thanks to their god, Dagon, for his capture, Samson asks to be placed between the pillars that support the building. He prays that he will be given back his strength one last time, so that he can bring down the building on the heads of his enemies, even if this will cost him his life. God hears his prayer and Samson dies among the rubble, along with all the Philistines.[17]

What are we to make of this story? In order to understand Biblical writings fully, it is important to realise that the Scriptures were not written in one go, so to speak, but composed over many centuries.[18] They therefore reflect a growing understanding on the part of the authors, and of their audience, of who God is and how he acts. This development also applies to attitudes to violence and its use. In the words of one commentator, 'God condemns every violent injustice. But He does it progressively, taking into account the age in which His people are living.'[19]

Since the time of Christ, we have the chance of a fuller understanding of how God wants us to live, so that the account of Samson's destruction of the Temple cannot be used as a justification for political violence today.

The story of the life of Samson refers to events that may have taken place in the tenth century BC. Some centuries later, the prophets began to speak of God, not as a warrior king, but as a gentle and peaceful God. In the words of the prophet Zechariah, who lived in the late fourth century BC, God was a king who was 'humble and riding on a donkey.'[20]

This was precisely how Jesus was to enter Jerusalem, as a humble king who did not seek to impose his reign by force. The example of Christ puts an end forever to the use of violence and killing as a means of achieving a goal and it is the model for all Christians and indeed every human being to follow.[21]

Direct Action in the New Testament?

Bearing in mind Christ's rejection of violence, there is one Gospel event which is difficult to explain. It is the passage where Christ ejects the traders and money-changers from the Jewish Temple in Jerusalem. There is much to say about this event, but here I want to concentrate on the fact that Christ was restoring the Temple to its proper use.

This is how the Gospel of St Matthew describes the scene,

> Jesus then went into the Temple and drove out all those who were selling and buying there. He upset the tables of the money-changers and the seats of the dove-sellers. He said to them, 'According to scripture, my house will be called a house of prayer, but you are turning it into a bandits' den'.[22]

The animals for sale were intended for Temple sacrifices, but they were not meant to be sold inside the sacred space, which was for worship only. The Jews did not fully understand Jesus' actions, but they would have known that the Jewish leader Nehemiah, who lived in the fifth century BC, had removed a family who had been given lodgings in some of the Temple rooms.[23]

Jesus' ejection of the traders is therefore not a way of imposing his will through violence. On the contrary, it serves the truth about the purpose of the Temple: 'My Father's house is a house of prayer, so do not use it for anything else.'

There is another aspect of this scene that it is particularly important to understand in our times. Christ's action is not rooted in his feelings, but in his awareness of the truth about the Temple and his zeal for its proper use.

Very often, nowadays, people believe that the mere fact of feeling strongly about something justifies a particular action. However, it is the truth about the situation that justifies the action, not the accompanying feelings: Christ is in his Father's house; he is the owner's Son; he therefore has the right to evict the intruders who have invaded it.

The ejection of the Temple traders by force is an isolated instance in the life of Christ. When the Jewish authorities came to arrest him, he would have had every right to defend himself, but he renounced the use of force.

The Apostle Peter, on the other hand, thought that now was the time to draw his sword to defend his Master. He therefore attacked one of the guards, cutting off his ear, but Jesus healed the man, saying to Peter,

> Put your sword back, for all who draw the sword will die by the sword. Or do you think that I cannot appeal to my Father, who would promptly send more than twelve legions of angels to my defence? But then, how would the scriptures be fulfilled that say this is the way it must be?

In the Temple, Christ restores his Father's house to its proper use. Outside the Temple, he meekly submits to those who have, for the time being, been given authority over him. He could have imposed his kingdom by force, but that would have contradicted the very nature of that kingdom. As we shall see later, when he stood before Pilate, Christ repeated what he had said to Peter, that he could have legions of angels fight for him, but that was not what he had chosen to do.[24]

Christians have had to learn to renounce violence again and again over the centuries; there have been times when they felt tempted, and even believed it their duty, to fight for the supremacy of their faith. In the Middle Ages there were many crusades to recapture the Holy Land from Muslim rule by military force. Even today, there are isolated instances of Christian anti-abortionists resorting to murder of abortion clinic staff, as an extreme means of imposing the teaching of the Church. There are also many well-documented cases of pro-abortion violence.[25] 'Put your sword back' (Mt 26:52) is addressed as much to us today as it was to Peter at the time of Christ.

The Roots of Terrorism

It is not possible to love one's neighbour as oneself, while planning to blow him up. Terrorism contradicts both the greatest commandment of the Law, about loving one's neighbour as oneself, and the commandment not to kill. However, terrorism can take root long before anyone plants a bomb or fires a shot. It begins in the heart of the person who becomes a terrorist, because angry thoughts can lead to angry words and on to violent actions. Jesus taught that it is not enough to avoid the actual killing; rather, it is necessary to reject the angry thoughts that can lead to killing. Also, there must be no shouting of the insults that are the outward expression of angry thoughts. 'If you call your brother a fool or an idiot, you will answer for it', he says.[26] By revealing the causes of violent actions,

Jesus goes far deeper than the original Old Testament commandment.

In a telling reflection, Pope Emeritus Benedict has shown what motivates anyone who despises human life. According to the Pope, violence can seem so attractive, because it 'is able to cloak itself in the semblance of morality'.[27] The use of violence then becomes part of a struggle for justice, so that a person who uses violence is sometimes praised as acting morally.

In this connection, I cannot help thinking of the many thrillers where the unfairly treated hero fights his way to justice with his fists and sometimes his gun. In these cases, his behaviour is usually portrayed as justified, because, despite acting outside the law, he has right on his side.

That does not mean that every time I feel angry about something, I am on the way to committing murder, because it is possible to reject the angry thoughts or to accept them. I have a choice. It is only the acceptance of such thoughts that leads to violence and that is the situation Jesus describes.

From Direct Action to Terrorism

The bitter fruits of angry thoughts that Jesus describes can be seen also in the developments from moderate direct action, to violent direct action, to terrorism that are all too common.

For instance, a particular group gets angry about a perceived injustice and feels it will never be heard through the ballot box or the courts. Members of the group then begin to take fairly mild action, such as sit-ins or noisy invasions of Parliament. If that does not achieve what they want, they may begin to damage public buildings or even the homes of people who disagree with them. At this point they may cross the line to terrorism by attacking or even killing their adversaries, so that they try to buy a perceived good life at the cost of the lives of others. Here we see clearly the line of development from angry thoughts, to words, to deeds.

The violence described in some parts of the Old Testament reflects an as yet imperfect understanding of the way God has called his followers to live and therefore cannot be used by Christians to justify violent behaviour today.

Conclusion: Terrorism as a Threat to Human Life

Terrorist acts are on the increase today, but the threat to human life they present is nowhere near as great as the risk posed by embryo destructions, abortions and also, to some extent, assisted dying. Nevertheless the threat to life from terrorism is growing not just with regard to the number of fatalities, but also to the expansion of the areas that are no longer considered safe from attacks.

Both direct activists and terrorists have lost faith in democracy, seeking instead to achieve their aims by various forms of pressure or violence. They may begin by seemingly innocuous activities such as interrupting a play, but in many cases they move on to throwing bombs in order to achieve their goals. There is thus a clear line of development from direct action to terrorism. Neither activists nor terrorists respect the privacy, the property or, in the most extreme cases, the lives of other people. Jesus has pointed to the anger felt in the heart as the source of all violent action and killing.

Although mainstream religions reject terrorism, acts of terror are carried out in their name by extremist minorities, thereby doing great harm to the moderate majorities.

Overall Summary

- The terrorist threat is similar to the other threats to human life that we have considered, because it destroys life for the sake of a particular goal.
- Terrorism is unlike the other threats to human life in that it tends to kill indiscriminately.
- Direct action is often the first step towards terrorism, as it seeks to force its views on others.
- Direct action is often used as a backup to democratic means of persuasion.
- Terrorism seeks to achieve its goals by force only.
- Terrorism is on the increase and has a high profile in the media, but it poses a much lower threat to human life than embryo destruction and abortion. Nevertheless, terrorism is on the increase.
- Some passages in Scripture appear to support direct action and terrorism, but closer examination does not bear this out.
- The attitude of terrorists is the exact opposite to that of Christ who never sought to impose his will on others.
- All the mainstream Christian Churches reject terrorism, as do most non-Christian religions.

Terrorism kills indiscriminately, but it is usually directed at particular groups of human beings, so that it shares some of the aims of eugenics. The next chapter will describe the attitudes that have led to selective breeding of human beings in the recent past, above all in Nazi Germany.

118   *A Good Life—At Any Price*

Notes

1. As reported by the BBC News 23 September 2013. http://www.bbc.co.uk/news/uk-england-24271396 (1 February 2014).
2. National Council for Voluntary Organizations, 'Participation: trends, facts and figures', London, March 2011, p. 41, Report by C. Saunders, Centre for Citizenship, Globalisation and Governance, University of Southampton. www.mcvo-vol.org.uk (1 December 2011).
3. *The Times*, 4 June 2007.
4. *The Times*, 4 March 2006.
5. 'The 2005 General Election in Great Britain', D. Sanders, H. Clarke, M. Stewart and P. Whiteley, Report for the Electoral Commission, August 2005, p. 4. www.essex.ac.uk/bes/Papers/ec%20report%20final.pdf (16 December 2011).
6. 'History and Government', 'US Elections', http://www.infoplease.com /ipa/A0781453.html (19 December 2011).
7. M. Begin, *The Revolt: The Story of Irgun* (London: WH Allen, 1951), p. 40.
8. Joint statement from Christians and Muslims in Britain, *Independent Catholic News*, 7 July 2005.
9. Jihad Against Jews and Crusaders: World Islamic Front Statement http://www.fas.org/irp/world/para/docs/980223-fatwa.htm (23 February 1998),and *Al-Jazeera*; 'Bin Laden tape obtained in Pakistan' ,http://msnbc.msn.com/id/6363306/, MSNBC, 30 October 2004. (7 September 2006).
10. J. Burke, *Al-Qaeda—The True Story of Radical Islam*, (London:I. B. Tauris, 2004), pp. 23, 162–3.
11. A. Taheri, *The Times*, 7 August 2005.
12. Joint statement from Christians and Muslims in Britain, *Independent Catholic News*, 7 July 2005.
13. *The Statistics Portal*, http://www.statistica.com/statistics /202871/number-of-fatalities-by-terrorist-attacks-worldwide/ (29 June 2015). For a lower estimate, see, http://www.nationmaster.com , based on 'MIPT Terrorism Knowledge Base'. (9 January 2012).
14. 2 S 5:17–25.
15. *The New Jerusalem Bible*, Standard Edition, (London:Darton,

Longman & Todd, 1985), Chronological Table p. 2056f.

16   Jg 13:5, 16:15–22.

17   Jg 16:29.

18   *The New Jerusalem Bible* speaks, very approximately, of the Bible covering datable events from Abraham (c. 1850 BC) to the time of the first Christians in the first century. See 'Introduction to the Pentateuch', p. 12 and Chronological Table p. 2073.

19   *Dictionary of Biblical Theology*, Second Edition Revised & Enlarged, Edited under the direction of X. Léon-Dufour, (London: Geoffrey Chapman, 1978). Entry for *violence*. The question of violence in the Bible is a complex one and it is worth reading the whole entry under 'violence' in the above work.

20   Zc 9:9.

21   *The New Jerusalem Bible,* notes pp. 276f and 1186.

22   Mt 21:12–13. See also Mk 11:15–18, Lk 19:45–46, Jn 2: 13–22.

23   Ne 13:7ff. See also *The New Jerusalem Bible*, 'Introduction to the Books of Chronicles, Ezra and Nehemiah', pp. 508–511 and Mt 26:52–54. See also Jn 18:10–11.

24   Jn 18:36.

25   See, for example, *The National Abortion Federation*, '2018 Violence and Disruption Statistics.' However, there are two sides to this story. Pro-life organization Human Life International (HLI) has documented cases of pro-abortion violence for years. Their research is published online at: http://abortion violence.com/ and on a blog titled: Tree in the Sea (see: http://tree-in-the-sea.blogspot.com/2008/05/pro-abortion-violence.html). The latter has a list that is over 100 pages long and contains more than 2,000 cases.

26   Mt 5:21–23.

27   J. Cardinal Ratzinger, *Co-Workers of the Truth*, (San Francisco: Ignatius Press, 1992), p. 264.

6 QUALITY CONTROL OF HUMAN LIFE

Selective Breeding in the Past and Present

I HAVE A CLOSE friend with a crippling inherited disease in the family. She herself is not affected, but she has told me of her sadness that a gifted grandchild of hers should have to live with such serious handicaps. 'It affects everyone', my friend said, 'and the poor girl can only expect to get worse.' The conversation then turned to ways of avoiding the disease and my friend said that it would have been better to use IVF to make sure that the embryo with the faulty gene was not implanted. This would, of course, have meant the death of that embryo.

Nevertheless, many people would agree with her. As we have seen in earlier chapters, the idea that no one should be born handicapped, or, more ominously, defective is gaining ground in ever-wider circles today. I believe that this idea is linked to the notion that everything we use in our lives should work. We therefore need quality control to avoid having to put up with rejects.

Quality control of things is all very well, but what happens when this practice is transferred to human beings? The idea may seem outrageous, but it is precisely what takes place when we discard so-called defective embryos, abort sick and unwanted unborn children and help handicapped people to die. The human being is then treated as a sub-standard product rather than a person.

There is a word for this kind of weeding out of the unfit. It is called *eugenics*, referring to a method of selective breeding of human beings which was popular in the late nineteenth and first half of the twentieth century, above all in Nazi Germany. Those who subscribe to this approach value human beings for their abilities and intelligence rather than for their humanity.

In this chapter we will outline some of the general ideas on which the eugenic practices of Nazi Germany were based in order to compare these with the threats to human life in our own times. It must be stressed that not all of what took place in the Third Reich is directly comparable with what is happening in our times, but there are enough similarities, particularly with regard to the treatment of the sick and handicapped, for a comparison to throw light on what is taking place today.

The crucial difference between the Nazi period and the present day is that, in the Third Reich, the eugenic measures were systematically imposed from above, whereas today they have been gradually introduced as a result of pressure from below, that is, from public opinion. Therefore, in our times, the responsibility for human life has to a great extent shifted from the state to the individual.

Eugenic Ideas in the Past: UK and US

The word *eugenics* was first used in 1883 by the British geneticist Sir Francis Galton. During the early years of the twentieth century, Galton wrote a series of publications on genetics, in which he sought to popularise and gain support for the concept of *eugenics*, that is, the systematic improvement of a species through selection or elimination of particular traits.

The idea of improving the race became popular in many countries, including the UK, the US and, above all, Nazi Germany. In the US, research into plant improvement through selective breeding led to an interest in comparable measures for humans. As a result, the idea began to take hold that the socially unfit, the criminal and those carrying hereditary diseases should be prevented from passing on their genes, in order to reduce poverty, crime and social unrest. The main tool advocated by supporters of the movement was the sterilisation of those considered unfit to breed. This idea was put into practice in the US and Nazi Germany, but not in the UK.

There was, however, a vigorous eugenics campaign in the UK, leading to the formation of the *Eugenics Education Society* in 1907.[1] When, a few years later, a member of this society asked Winston Churchill, then British Home Secretary, whether he would support measures to discourage the 'feeble-minded' and other 'degenerate types' from becoming parents, he gave a startling reply. He said that these people deserved, 'all that could be done for them ... now that they were in the world', but that they should be segregated, so that 'their curse died with them and was not transmitted to future generations.'[2]

Churchill is reported as having said privately that the fact that the mentally deficient tended to have more children than those of greater intelligence was 'a very terrible danger to the race.'[3] With these words Churchill undoubtedly expressed the prevalent opinion not only in the UK, but in many other countries too.

In the US a growing belief in the necessity of eugenic measures led to some fifteen states passing sterilisation laws between 1907 and 1917; later fifteen more were to introduce similar legislation. As a result, 'habitual or confirmed criminals' and persons guilty of serious crimes such as rape, could now be forcibly sterilised.[4] In total, more than 60,000 sterilisations were carried out between 1907 and 1963 and some states continued to sterilise into the 1970s.[5]

Nazi Germany

The number of sterilisations in the US may seem large, but they are as nothing compared with the 350,000 compulsory sterilisations carried out in Nazi Germany between 1934 and 1945.[6] Over a period of only ten years the Reich had succeeded in making far more people incapable of having children than the US had been able to in over half a century.

Nevertheless, the number of sterilisations in the US had been large enough to make an impression on contemporary German eugenicists. In 1925, eight years before Hitler came to power, German officials contacted individual US state governments, asking for information about the American sterilisation laws. A leading advocate of eugenics in Germany commented on the American replies with these telling words,

> What we racial hygienists promote is not at all new or unheard of. In a cultural nation of the first order, the United States of America, that which we strive toward was introduced long ago. It is all so clear and simple.[7]

In other words, 'We do not stand alone', as one Nazi propaganda poster put it, showing the flags of all the countries which had introduced eugenic measures, including the US.[8]

Nazi thinking had been strongly influenced by a German tract entitled *Authorization of the Destruction of Life Unworthy of Life*, published jointly in 1920 by a lawyer and a psychiatrist. The authors argued that 'incurable idiots' could not suffer so that there was no reason to have compassion with them or to respect their right to life. They also argued that, from an economic standpoint, such people were simply a burden to the state.

Some twelve years later, Hitler's government took up these arguments to justify the killing of psychiatric patients and others thought unworthy of life.[9] However, they began by introducing the forced sterilisation of those considered unsuitable for propagating the race. It was 'all so clear and simple.'

Sterilisation

The sterilisation laws, introduced a few months after Adolf Hitler was appointed Chancellor in January 1933, were only the first step in a programme to 'improve the German Aryan Breed'. The new government planned to cleanse the German nation of all 'inferior' elements, so as to create the ideal pan-German society.[10] Special 'Health Inheritance Courts' with medical personnel as judges were therefore set up all over Germany.[11] A large part of the work of these courts concerned the removal of anyone of Jewish descent, but they also dealt with cases of people with an inheritable physical or mental disease or defect, which is the aspect of the legislation that interests us here.

Under the threat of severe penalties, doctors and psychiatrists were required to refer patients who might be 'unfit to breed' to the authorities. As we have seen, by the end of the Second World War, over 350,000 individuals had been sterilised under this law.[12]

It is true that, unlike abortion, sterilisation does not put an end to a human life. However, it does prevent a human life from being created. As a result, it easily becomes the first step towards abortion as well as euthanasia.

Abortion

This next step was indeed taken when the sterilisation law was amended in 1935 to allow for eugenic abortions to prevent the 'genetically unfit' from having children.[13] It is unclear how many such abortions were carried out, but, according to one source, there were some 7,000 while Hitler was in power.[14] These abortions provide a clear parallel with similar abortions in today's society.

Forced Euthanasia of Handicapped Children and Adults

Sterilisation and abortion were only the first steps in the campaign to cleanse the German people of those considered unfit to breed or to live. In 1939 a more sinister development took place. The Ministry of the Interior issued a decree requiring medical personnel to report all cases of children born with physical or mental defects. The intention was to kill such infants early in life, so that they could not grow up to have defective children.

During 1939 more than 5,000 children up to sixteen were put to death as part of this eugenic programme, though sometimes the deaths were disguised as 'natural'.[15] The disguise may have been used because there was some shame associated with the programme. However, it is equally possible, and perhaps more plausible, that those involved wanted to ensure that no one prevented them from carrying out their plans.

An even greater cloak of secrecy was cast over the euthanasia programme for adults considered 'unfit to live'. Although Hitler had authorised the programme in a personal note in 1939, euthanasia remained officially illegal throughout the Nazi period. The adult euthanasia operation was run from a headquarters in Berlin, but affected adults from asylums throughout Germany. According to one source, some 70,000 mentally handicapped and chronically sick adults were killed in Germany between 1940 and 1941 (for instance by gassing and lethal injections).

Although Hitler, in his authorisation of the adult euthanasia programme, described such deaths as a *Gnadentod*, a 'merciful death', the scheme could not by any stretch of the imagination be described as merciful. Rather, it was a ruthless and systematic disposal of some of the weakest members of society.[16]

The Handicapped as a Financial Burden

In order to support its programme of eradicating inherited diseases, the Nazi government sought to instil the idea into the general population that people suffering from inherited diseases were not only unfit to breed, but were also an intolerable financial burden on able-bodied citizens. For instance, one poster showed a healthy, blonde German bent under a yoke on which sat two sick men, one of them made to look like an ape. The text read, 'You too are carrying this burden. A person with an inherited disease costs on average 50,000 *Reichsmark* by the time he is 60.' The implication was that he had contributed nothing to society during that time.[17] Such propaganda was in tune with much public opinion in the world at the time, but also with some public opinion today. Think of the not uncommon attitude to the birth of a Downs Syndrome baby that, 'surely, she could have had the test', with the implication that she should have aborted the child.

Eugenics in Decline

Outside Nazi Germany the enthusiasm for eugenics was already in decline before the Second World War broke out. The economic depression in the late twenties and early thirties had been a strong contributory factor to this, especially in the US, because it revealed that everyone, not just the sick and the social misfits, was hit by the bad times.

Since the whole eugenics movement had been based on the idea that society could be improved by breeding out 'degenerates' of various kinds, the fact that it was not only those who were affected by the economic downturn discredited the whole movement.[18]

The other, and probably more decisive, reason for the decline in support for eugenics was that the full horror of Hitler's mass killings in the extermination camps became known after the War. Not all of these killings had a eugenic purpose, but the fact that human beings, any human beings, could be treated in this way made a powerful impact. Even in its milder form of sterilisation, the practice came to be too closely associated with the atrocities of Hitler's time in office to be acceptable in any form in the immediate post-war years. However, eugenic ideas did not disappear; they remained dormant, only to re-emerge some twenty years later in new forms.

The Re-Emergence of Eugenic Threats

The fundamental idea behind all kinds of eugenics is a desire to control the development of the human race. In Nazi Germany this took the form of a systematic eradication both of specific ethnic groups and of the sick and handicapped. Eugenic measures were imposed by the government and mainly enforced via the judicial system. If they wished to avoid a prison sentence, Germans of those times had to obey the legislation.

In our times, eugenics has re-emerged as a result of pressure from public opinion, often based on compassion for sick and handicapped people. The thinking behind this form of compassion, if it is compassion, is that no one should be born with, or have to live with, a serious disability or illness. This idea is now so widely accepted that it has led to the legalisation of the practices described in this book in an increasing number of countries. Diseased embryos and unborn children are destroyed before they can grow to maturity and many handicapped and sick adults campaign for assisted suicide or euthanasia.

In the Netherlands there is even pressure for the right to euthanasia for people who are simply tired of life or who fear the future effects of a degenerative disease. In a previous chapter we have spoken of a Dutch girl in her twenties who was granted euthanasia, precisely because of such a fear. She sought to control her life by ending it at a moment of her choosing.

These threats to human life have developed so slowly that we may not have understood fully what is taking place. Also, with our choice of words we often seek to hide, even from ourselves, the fact that we now take life for the sake of a good life.

Words as Disguise

Let us look in more detail at some of the words used about the deliberate ending of a human life. For instance, if we say that Peter killed Mary, then that is a neutral description of what took place. If, on the other hand, we say that Peter helped Mary to die, then we have said something important about our attitude to the killing, because we now imply that Peter did a good deed by killing her.

Something comparable takes place with the words we use about an *abortion*. The word itself simply means a 'miscarriage', but, in contemporary usage, it has come to mean 'an artificially induced miscarriage'. However, the form a doctor fills in to sanction an abortion uses the letters 'TOP' which mean 'Termination of Pregnancy'. These words say nothing about the fact that an unborn child will be removed from the womb and die; rather, they state that the woman will no longer have a condition called *pregnancy*.

At an early abortion the mother is given medication to cause the unborn child to be expelled from the womb. At a late abortion, the doctor kills the child in the womb, after which the dead body is delivered. However, the vocabulary used about these events safely distance those involved from the reality of what takes place.

This distancing is even more pronounced when it comes to embryo destruction. Here the talk is of *selection* for implantation and *destruction* of embryos that are either considered defective or that are carriers of inherited abnormalities. As we have seen, the embryo is a human being from the moment of conception, which means that large numbers of very young humans are regularly killed, some of them for eugenic reasons. I do not think the words used in connection with the killing of embryos are intended to mislead; they reflect the fact that many of those involved do not believe the embryo is a human being.

The term *euthanasia* means an 'easy death', which is what people seek with the various forms of *assisted dying*. Such a death can sound like a merciful escape from unbearable pain and illness, but it masks the fact that one person kills another or helps another to kill himself. In Hitler's Germany, it was called a *merciful death*, but it always involved killing a sick person against their will and it was always done for eugenic reasons. This ought to be a warning to those campaigning for the right to assisted dying.

The words that describe an action can help to conceal what is actually taking place, but we cannot close our eyes to reality forever. Another person's moment of truth may help to shake us out of our complacency, so that we see things as they really are.

Moment of Truth: The Diaries of a German Officer

In Nazi Germany many people closed their eyes or were ignorant of what was happening to their fellow human beings. In this situation, some sleepwalked towards co-operating with an ever greater threat to human life, while others, such as the teacher Wilm Hosenfeld, heard a wake-up call which made them face the truth.

Hosenfeld was conscripted into the German army during the Second World War and stationed in Warsaw in occupied Poland. Throughout this period, he kept a number of diaries which he managed to send back to his family in Germany. These tell of his increasing disillusionment with the Nazi regime and his horror at what was being done to the Jewish population in Poland.

By posting them, he was taking a considerable risk, as the content would undoubtedly have been viewed as treasonous by the censors. The family also took a risk by keeping material that might have sent them to a concentration camp if it had been discovered. However, both Hosenfeld and his family must have thought the risks worth taking, so that the diaries might one day be made known to the world.

A particularly poignant extract describes what happened to some of the newborn children in the Warsaw ghetto in 1942,

> ... a woman told [a Polish acquaintance of mine] that several Gestapo made their way into the Jewish maternity hospital, took the babies away, put them in a sack, went off and threw them into a hearse. These wicked men were unmoved by the crying of the infants and their mothers' heart-rending wails ...

> What cowards we are, thinking ourselves above all
> this, but letting it happen. We shall be punished
> for it too, ... for we are colluding when we allow
> these crimes to be committed.[19]

For Hosenfeld, hearing this account was a moment of truth. He came to see the killing of the Jewish babies as a symbol of the wholesale destruction of human life under Nazi rule. He also understood that, if ordinary Germans like himself did not speak out against these atrocities, they would bear some of the responsibility for the killings.

He never had the opportunity to tell the world what he had come to believe. After the defeat of Germany, he was taken prisoner by the Soviet army and died in Russian captivity seven years later. However, his act of courage in sending the diaries back was not in vain, because, after the War, his family were able to publish his words, so that they can speak to us too.

The action of the Gestapo on that terrible day in 1942 has the capacity to shock us, because we see the poor children in our minds' eyes and we hear the screams of the mothers. Surely, something like that could never happen now, could it?

There is a sense in which it is already happening in our own times. If we could see the unborn children who are aborted and the embryos who are thrown away as the human beings they really are, would we not shrink in horror and be as shocked as we are by the killing of the Jewish babies?

Hosenfeld's words are a wake-up call for us today, who count ourselves civilised. We, too, need to speak our minds about the destruction of so many young human lives.

It is true that those involved do not always understand what they are doing or allowing to be done. That is why it is

Quality Control of Human Life   133

so important to expose the reality behind the words in common use about the practices threatening human life today.

Conclusion

With the account of the Fall of Adam and Eve, the biblical author sought to describe the fundamental damage that took place, when the first human beings tried to put themselves in God's place. Not only did they seek to take charge of their own lives, they also tried to remove people who were in their way. The first example of the new disorder is the murder of Abel by his brother Cain, but we see its effect down the ages, even in our own times.

During the Nazi period, less than a hundred years ago, there was a concerted effort to re-make the German people in the image of the Nazi ideal, that is, blonde, blue-eyed and free of any inherited disease or handicap. These human paragons were to be created through the systematic killing of those not fitting this model, whether in the womb, at birth or later in life. As the new laws were imposed by the state, individual Germans had to comply with them.

In our own times, there have been comparable developments. However, they now take place in the name of personal freedom and the right to choose. Those affected are mainly embryos and unborn children, though more and more countries are also legalising the killing of seriously ill and handicapped people who want to die. There are even signs that some of these measures are imposed, if not by the state, then by the medical personnel involved.

Most of these changes are hailed as signs of progress in individual freedom, but they are all based on a subjective choice rather than the objective truth about the right to life of everyone. What is more, they have taken place so slowly and gradually that it can be difficult to see what is actually happening and where it may all be leading.

On the other hand, events in Nazi Germany took place over a relatively short period of time, so that they can provide us with a clearer picture of what may occur in our times, if we continue to treat some human beings as expendable.

On a basis of this picture and what has already taken place in the UK, the US and, above all, in the Netherlands, it is possible to make some tentative predictions about future risks to human life.

We can expect that ever-increasing numbers of human beings will be subjected to quality control. This could take the form of prospective parents being tested for genetically transmitted diseases and handicaps and being required to use PGD (diagnosing a faulty gene before implantation) to avoid transmitting the genetic fault. Mothers expecting a handicapped child might also be coerced into aborting it.

In the case of PVS patients and others thought to be unable to decide for themselves, it may become increasingly common to switch off their life support, because their quality of life is considered too low.

In this connection, it is significant that Germany, along with Austria, is one of the few countries that is currently introducing legislation to ban all forms of euthanasia. In those countries, at least, people have not forgotten the systematic slaughter of those considered 'unworthy of life' by the Nazi regime.[20]

The destruction of embryos, unborn children and the various forms of assisted dying all point towards a society where only fit and healthy people are considered full members of the community. It is true that these measures are not (yet) imposed from above, but, unless the current trend is reversed, even that step cannot be ruled out at some point in the future.

Wilm Hosenfeld wanted to urge the German people to protest against the systematic destruction of human life in his time, but he did not have the chance to make his appeal public. We, on the other hand, are free to speak out against the life-destroying practices of today, even if, like my friend with the inherited disease, we are sometimes tempted to destroy life for the sake of a healthy life.

Overall Summary

- Hitler came to power in an international climate of approval for eugenic ideas.
- The Nazi regime took eugenic measures to extremes by systematically killing those deemed 'unworthy of life.'
- The most striking similarity between the Nazi period and our own times is the legal destruction of specific categories of human life.
- The most important difference is that today legislation is enacted as a result of pressure from public opinion, not imposed by the state.
- The threat to human life today is many times greater than that of Nazi Germany.
- Embryos and unborn children are now regularly killed for eugenic reasons.
- The slow growth of the threat today can blind us to what is happening.
- The rapid development of the threat in Nazi Germany can open our eyes to contemporary dangers to life.

Despite the official propaganda about 'mercy killings', eugenic killings in Nazi Germany were carried out because certain categories of people were considered unworthy of life. In contemporary society the motivation for such killings is often compassion for suffering people or the desire to prevent someone from being born with a handicap. Nevertheless, in both societies, certain groups were and are considered expendable. The methods used in Nazi Germany were those of a dictatorship rather than a democracy, but the thinking behind the destruction of human life was not so different. Therein lies the danger to contemporary society, but also the challenge to protect all human life and this will be the subject of the next chapters.

Notes

1   D. J. Kevles, *In the Name of Eugenics, Genetics and the Uses of Human Heredity* (Cambridge:Harvard University Press, 1999), p. 98ff.

2   As quoted in Kevles, *In the Name of Eugenics*, p. 98.

3   As quoted in Kevles, *In the Name of Eugenics*, p. 99.

4   Kevles, *In the Name of Eugenics*, p. 100.

5   A. Stern, Eugenic Nation: Faults and Frontiers of Better Breeding in Modern America, (Berkeley, University of California Press, 2005), pp. 84, 224.

6   'Eugenics: Compulsory sterilization in 50 American States', research project by L. Kaelber, University of Vermont. http://www.uvm.edu/~lkaelber/eugenics/ (25 January 2012).

7   J. Beckwith, 'Social and Political Uses of Genetics in the US: Past and Present' *in Annals of the US Academy of Science* (1976), p. 47. As quoted *in* J. Rifkin, *The Biotech Century*, (London:Victor Gollanzc, 1998), p. 126.

8   See A. Spiegel, 'The Jeremiah Metzger Lecture: a Brief History of Eugenics in America: Implications for Medicine in the 21st Century' in *Transactions of the American Clinical and Climatological Association* 130(2019) pp. 216–234.

9   K. Binding and A. Hoche, *Die Freigabe der Vernichtung lebensunwerten Lebens*, (*Authorization of the Destruction of Life Unworthy of Life)*, (Leipzig:Meiner, 1920). As referred to in M. Burleigh, 'Nazi "Euthanasia" Programs' *in Deadly Medicine*, ed. D. Kuntz and S. Bachrach, United States Holocaust Memorial Museum, Washington D.C. 2004, S. J. Bloomfield, p. 128.

10   'Racial Policy of Nazi Germany', http://en.wikipedia.org/

wiki/Racial_policy_of_Nazi_Germany (4 January 2011) and 'The Nuremberg Laws (1933–35)', (Translation of full text) http://teachers.sduhsd.net/mmontgomery/world_history/totalitarianism_ww2/laws.htm (4 January 2011).

11 M. Burleigh, 'Nazi "Euthanasia" Programs' *in Deadly Medicine*, ed. D. Kuntz and S. Bachrach, United States Holocaust Memorial Museum, (Washington D.C.:Bloomfield, 2004), p. 131.

12 H. J. Winckelmann and M. Bitschi 'Implementation of the Law Intended to Prevent Hereditary Diseases at the Heilig-Geist-Spital, Ravensburg'. Paper given at the 40th International Congress on the History of Medicine, Budapest 2006, p. 2. http://www.ishm2006.hu/scientific/abstract.php?ID=73 (17 January 2008).

13 I. Richter, *Katholizismus und Eugenik in der Weimarer Republik und im Dritten Reich: Zwischen Sittlichkeitsreform un Rassenhygiene* (Catholicism and Eugenics in the Weimar Republic and in the Third Reich: Between a Reform in Morality and Racial Hygiene), (Paderborn:Schoeningh. 2001), p. 489. As quoted by J. Glad *in Mankind Quarterly*, vol. 46, No. 4, Summer, 2006, ,pp. 497–507.

14 *Deadly Medicine*, ed. D. Kuntz and S. Bachrach, United States Holocaust Memorial Museum, (Washington D.C.: Bloomfield, 2004), p. 202.

15 M. Burleigh, 'Nazi "Euthanasia" Programs' *in Deadly Medicine*, ed. D. Kuntz and S. Bachrach, United States Holocaust Memorial Museum, (Washington D.C:Bloonfield, 2004), p. 134.

16 M. Burleigh, 'Nazi "Euthanasia" Programs' *in Deadly Medicine*, ed. D. Kuntz and S. Bachrach, United States Holocaust Memorial Museum, (Washington D.C: Bloomfield,2004), pp. 131–139.

17 M. Burleigh, 'Nazi "Euthanasia" Programs' *in Deadly Medicine*, ed. D. Kuntz and S. Bachrach, United States Holocaust Memorial Museum, (Washington D.C:Bloomfield, 2004), p. 126.

18 J. Rifkin, *The Biotech Century*, (London: Victor Gollancz, 1998), p. 126.

19 'Extracts from the Diary of Captain W. Hosenfeld', entry for 13th August 1942. Published in W. Szpilman *The Pianist*, (London:Orion Books, 2002), p. 199f.

20 *The Tablet*, 22 February 2014.

PART II

PROTECTING
HUMAN LIFE

INTRODUCTION TO PART II

THE UNIVERSAL INSTINCT to protect human life can make itself felt even in quite small children. Recently the TV news reported an item about a little girl of two or three who had called the emergency services when her pregnant mother collapsed in front of her. The girl managed to get to the phone, dial the right number and then had a perfectly sensible conversation with the woman the other end; after this it did not take long for an ambulance to arrive. Both mother and baby survived and the programme showed the girl being given an award for her bravery. She had saved the lives not only of her mother, but of her unborn sibling.

This very young child was probably exceptional, but the urge to help someone in danger is something fundamentally human. 'I couldn't have done anything else', is a comment one often hears after a person is praised for an act of bravery.

Until not so long ago, the protection of all innocent human life was enshrined in the legislation of most countries. However, in our times, there are more and more state-sanctioned threats to human life, especially at its beginning and end. The threats at the beginning of life are due to the widespread belief that the embryo and unborn child do not have the same right to life as human beings after birth. At the end of life, the threat is due to the belief that the sick and disabled have the right to die, if they are suffering unbearably.

The State, in the West at least, still protects most human lives, but the protection of the most vulnerable human beings is increasingly left to religious bodies, above all the Catholic Church, and the conscience of individuals. In practice this means that there is a growing gap between much national and international legislation and Church teaching. In the following three chapters, we will consider the implications of this gap for individuals and for society in general.

In the chapter on legislation and Catholic teaching, we show how the right to life of all, which is enshrined in the UN *Declaration of Human Rights* and expressed in most national legislations, is gradually being eroded by a right to destroy life at its beginning and end. We also show that the introduction of this type of legislation has led to conflicts with Catholic-run hospitals, particularly in Ireland and the US. The opposition between Church and State affects individual health care workers too, as they are faced with increasingly difficult decisions, especially about co-operating in abortions.

Ordinary Catholics, too, must make choices about the many procedures to end life that are now legal. In the chapter on suffering and a good life, we describe what such decisions can mean for individual men and women.

In the final chapter, we consider in practical terms what a society that includes everyone might look like. We point to signs of hope for all the groups now under threat and show that these threats are expressions of despair. Only by choosing the path of hope will we be able to achieve the good life that we all desire.

7 LEGISLATION AND CATHOLIC TEACHING

WHENEVER THERE IS a major natural disaster or accident, countries from all over the world come together with the single aim of saving as many lives as possible, regardless of politics or religion. The mining accident in Northern Chile in 2010 was a particularly poignant example of such co-operation. Thirty-three workers were trapped underground after a cave-in in a copper mine and initially it was thought impossible that anyone could survive.

However, the miners managed to get a message to the surface, saying that they were safe and well. After this, the international community pooled its resources to get them out alive. During the sixty nine days it took to rescue the men, the whole world was watching and praying and once the last man had come to the surface, the world rejoiced that so many lives had been saved. At such a moment we all understand that nothing is more precious than life itself.

Nevertheless, the inherent value of every human being is regularly disregarded in connection with particular groups. In the previous chapter, we saw that handicapped people and others, above all Jews, were killed on a colossal scale in Nazi Germany. Those targeted were no longer considered fully human, so that they lost the right to live. Sadly we see something comparable in our times, despite efforts to protect human life better.

Never Again: the UN and Human Rights

Once the atrocities carried out during the Second World War, especially in Nazi Germany and the Japanese prison camps, had become known, there was a concerted effort to ensure that such things could never happen again. To this end, the UN was founded immediately after the War, in 1945. The purpose of the organisation was set out in the Preamble to its Charter which stated that the founding nations were determined to 'save succeeding generations from the scourge of war' and to 'reaffirm fundamental human rights.'[1] In order to achieve the latter, they drew up the *Universal Declaration of Human Rights.*

This document sought to express a common under-standing of human rights and it was, at least in theory, a significant step forward for the protection of human life.[2] The description of the *Declaration* as 'universal' is impor-tant, because that meant that the rights it contained belonged to everyone without exception; in the words of the document 'everyone has the right to life'.[3]

However, some twenty years after the ratification of the *Declaration*, most member states have begun to legalise practices that threaten human life at its beginning and end. In particular, the right to abortion is now taken for granted in many countries. If the unborn child was originally included in the 'everyone' who had the right to life, then that child certainly no longer has this automatic right. Without a definition of who 'everyone' refers to, it is impossible to protect the rights of all human beings.

Who is 'Everyone'?

As the UN has not provided a definition of what it means by 'everyone', the word could equally well mean 'everyone in the world' and 'every human being from conception onwards.' The UN *Convention on the Rights of the Child* of 1989 gives a hint that the latter definition might be implied, because it states that,

> the child ... needs special safeguards and care, including appropriate legal protection, before as well as after birth.[4]

Such protection would obviously include the unborn child's right to life.[5] However, the *Convention* does not specify how long before birth the child has this right, whether it is from conception, from viability or from some other point. The document is therefore open to a range of interpretations, only one of which implies that the child has the right to life from conception onwards. Because of this vagueness, the document in reality gives very limited protection to the child before birth.

The UN and Abortion Rights

More recent UN documents and pronouncements have weakened the right to life before birth contained in the 1989 *Convention*. Thus, in 2011, a report on health as a human right demanded that states must provide access to legal and safe abortion services.[6] The report claimed that lack of access to abortion infringed women's human rights.

In 2012 the UN Secretary General, Ban Ki-Moon, said, in an address to the UN Commission on Population and Development, that universal abortion rights must be extended to apply to young people too.[7]

These official UN calls for universal access to abortion mean that, in the case of the unborn child, the right to life of all is overridden by a presumed right to destroy the child, if that is what the mother wants.[8]

Far from ensuring that the many deliberately inflicted deaths of the Second World War would never be repeated, the organisation set up specifically to protect human life has in reality come to support the right to take the lives of unborn children on a scale comparable to that of the total number of deaths during that War.

The UN and Euthanasia

As euthanasia is now legal in many countries, the UN has been unable to agree on a general resolution condemning it. However, it has directed strong criticism at the country where the practice is most widely available, the Netherlands. In particular, the UN has described as unacceptable the fact that cases of euthanasia and assisted suicide in that country are reviewed only after the death of the patients.[9]

The organisation has urged the Netherlands to re-examine its laws to ensure that cases were reviewed before the patients were killed or helped to die, since mistakes obviously could not be rectified afterwards. Particular concern was expressed about the use of euthanasia involving minors and handicapped newborns.

These recommendations highlight both the capability and the limitations of the UN. The organisation was able to 'urge' a member state to change its legislation in order to protect human life, but it was not able to compel it to do so.

UN Protection of Human Life against Terrorism

In spite of the fact that the *Universal Declaration of Human Rights* was agreed specifically to avoid barbarous acts being carried out in the future, the UN has not been able to agree on a general definition of terrorism. A draft definition describes it as the unlawful killing or injuring of individuals or populations 'in order to compel a government or an international organisation to do or abstain from doing any act.'[10] This definition covers the most fundamental aspects of terrorism, above all its lack of respect for human life, but, because the Organisation of the Islamic Conferences wants it to exclude the acts of national liberation movements, member states have been unable to agree a common definition.[11] This difference of opinion highlights the fact that one person's terrorist is all too often another person's freedom fighter.

In its attempts to protect all human life and ensure a good life for everyone the UN is hampered at every turn by a lack of general agreement about when human life begins and which human lives should be protected.

State and National Legislation to Protect Human Life

The dominant trend in most countries, including the UK and the US, is towards a decline in protection for human life before birth and for the disabled and seriously ill, while those between these two extremes tend to be well protected. However, there are exceptions to the scant protection for some human lives.

The Embryo as a Juridical Person

In most countries, legal protection for the embryo, if it exists at all, relates to the rights of the parents rather than the embryonic child.

The legislation of the state of Louisiana provides a notable exception to this lack of protection, because the embryo is considered not as a piece of property, but as a *juridical person*, that is, a legal entity with its own rights. Louisiana legislation specifies that,

> An in vitro fertilised human ovum is a biological human being which is not the property of the physician which acts as an agent of fertilisation, or

the facility which employs him or the donors of the
sperm and ovum.[12]

Legally speaking, a *juridical person* is not a *person* in the
usual sense of a human being, but an entity, such as a firm,
which has been created by law and given a distinct identity.
Crucially for the embryo, however, a *juridical person* has
rights and therefore cannot be treated as a piece property
which can be disposed of at will.

According to Louisiana law, the parents of the embryo
have 'a high duty of care' for the embryo, but they can give
him or her up for adoption by another couple, if they so
wish. Before the adoption, the physician involved becomes
the temporary guardian of the embryo. Although the state
of Louisiana has not taken the final step of considering the
embryo an independent human being, its legislation
nevertheless treats it with a level of respect similar to that
granted to humans later in life.

The precarious situation of the embryo in other US
states can best be illustrated through the court cases that
can arise when a divorcing couple disagree about the
treatment of the frozen embryos they have created.

In one such case the husband wanted the embryos
implanted in a surrogate mother in order to give them a
chance of life. The wife argued that this would violate her
right to control her procreative decisions. She therefore
wanted the embryos destroyed. The court found in her
favour, stating that if her biological children were allowed to
be born, this could have life-long psychological repercussions
for her. It therefore ordered the embryos to be destroyed.

It is interesting that the court did not consider the
comparable repercussions on the husband of the destruction of the entities he believed were his children. In other
US court cases there has also been a tendency to favour the
right not to procreate above the protection of the embryos.

With the exception of Louisiana, US states have been reluctant to grant any independent rights to the embryo.[13]

Irish Law and The Unborn Child

In most of the countries we have looked at the unborn child has only limited legal protection. Until recently, Irish law formed an important exception to this lack of protection, because the right to life of the unborn was enshrined in the Irish Constitution. However, since the child in the womb and the mother had equal rights to life in Irish law, difficulties arose in cases where the mother's life was at risk from the pregnancy. After a number of court battles, the Irish Supreme Court ruled in 1992 that, in such cases, women had the right to an abortion. The legislation on the right to life of the unborn still stood, but the court ruling had in effect stated that, when the interests of the mother and the child conflicted, the mother took precedence over the child.[14]

Nevertheless, even in such cases, doctors were reluctant to perform abortions, because the 150 year-old *Offences against the Person Act*, making it an offence punishable by life imprisonment to destroy an unborn child, remained in force. Doctors were therefore afraid that they would prosecuted, if they agreed abort a child.

In 2010 there was a further development in the drama of Irish abortion legislation. Three Irishwomen who had gone to England to have abortions brought a case against the Irish State before the European Court of Human Rights (ECHR). All three women had suffered severe bleeding afterwards, but, because of the attitude to abortion in Ireland, they had found it difficult to get treatment, once they returned home. They claimed that current Irish abortion legislation violated the European Convention on

Human Rights, which establishes a right to respect for 'family and private life'.[15]

The ECHR ruled that this right did not mean that a woman was entitled to an abortion, but she did have a right to medical treatment to save her life and to information about such treatment. The Court found that the Irish State had failed to provide this information, awarding one of the women financial compensation.

In response to the ECHR ruling, the Irish State enacted the *Protection of Life during Pregnancy Act* in 2013, which included provision for a patient information leaflet for pregnant women as well as legalising abortion if the mother's life was in danger. After this, the ECHR closed the case.

The Act did not substantially change the level of protection for the unborn child in Ireland, but it did place on the statute book the right to an abortion in cases of danger to the mother's life, a right that had previously only been expressed in the Supreme Court ruling of 1992.[16] Following a referendum in 2018 the protection of the unborn child in Ireland was further weakened so as to allow early abortions in a range of cases.

Protection of Human Life: Catholic Perspectives

Religious denominations cannot protect human life in the same way as the law of the land. They can only seek to influence legislation through their teaching, through the services they run (especially hospitals) and through the formation of individual consciences. As we have seen in previous chapters, most religions respect human life at every stage, though there is some uncertainty about the status of the unborn child and, especially, the embryo.

Church Teaching

The Catholic Church has responded to the failure of national legislations to protect human life by publishing a number of teaching documents. These include Pope John Paul II's *The Gospel of Life* (*Evangelium Vitae*), which we have referred to many times in previous chapters. Significantly, the document is addressed not only to the Church, but to 'all people of good will', so that it seeks to reach out to the whole world, not just to members of the Catholic Church.[17]

The words of the Pope are a forceful reminder of biblical and Church teaching on the infinite value of all human life. In particular, he speaks of the many new threats to life, both at its beginning and at its end, that characterise our times. He mentions 'false and deceptive solutions' to medical problems that are now built into the health care systems of many countries. He points out that, because 'solutions' such as abortion and assisted suicide have gradually become socially acceptable, conscience itself has been damaged; so that it is now increasingly difficult for individuals to distinguish between right and wrong in relation to human life.[18]

Those who do seek to respect human life often find themselves in conflict with the state about the various procedures that are now legal in most countries. The conflict affects Catholic hospitals and health care personnel as well as many ordinary Catholics and it is most marked in countries where the Church runs hospitals, such as Ireland and the US.

Irish Hospitals and Church Teaching

Until recently, Ireland was considered one of the most Catholic countries in the world, but once the legislation permitting abortion in some cases had been passed, Irish

Catholic hospitals found themselves faced with a stark choice: They could obey the law, while disregarding the teaching of the Church, or they could follow Church teaching and risk state sanctions.

Of the twenty five hospitals named by the Irish state as 'appropriate institutions' to perform abortions, two are Catholic-run. After consulting the government about the new legislation, the board of one of these, the *Mater Misericordiae* in Dublin, was told that, while individuals had the right to conscientious objection about performing an abortion, institutions did not. In response, a member of the board said that this distinction amounted to a violation of the right of an institution to have an ethos. In the meantime, the hospital authorities stated that it would comply with the law.[19] At the time of writing, the Archbishop of Dublin, Diarmuid Martin, was still seeking clarification of the position of the hospital in relation to the law. The other Catholic hospital, the *St Vincent's* in Dublin, said that it would comply with the legislation.

A prominent Catholic barrister, Brett Lockhart, has commented that, if the state was going to force a Catholic hospital to compromise its fidelity to the teaching of the Church, it would be better to give the hospital to the state rather than cause confusion about something as fundamental as the right to life.[20]

US Hospitals and Church Teaching

The position of the many Catholic hospitals in the US on abortion is more clear-cut than that of those in Ireland. In the US, Catholic hospitals follow the guidance given by the US Bishops' *Ethical and Religious Directives*, which means that they do not perform abortions under any circumstances.

Because of this firm stance, the *American Civil Liberties Union*, an organisation whose purpose is to defend the rights and liberties of Americans, has brought a lawsuit against the *United States Conference of Catholic Bishops* on behalf of a woman who was refused an abortion. The *Union*'s case is that the Bishops' *Directives* conflict with the healthcare rights of women in the US and that the Bishops are therefore ultimately responsible for the failure of Catholic hospitals to provide emergency abortions.

The woman concerned in the law suit, Tamesha Means, was admitted to a Catholic hospital (the only hospital within reach), following pregnancy complications at eighteen weeks. She was not informed of the possibility of an abortion and was sent home, because the doctors said there was nothing more they could do for her. She was eventually re-admitted to the hospital, where she miscarried.

The *Union* contested that Mrs Means was made to suffer unnecessarily due to the hospital's anti-abortion policy. On 30 June 2015 the Michigan District Court dismissed the lawsuit, stating that a resolution of the case would involve 'reviewing religious doctrine.' The next day the *Union* appealed. The case is still on-going.[21]

The issue of the healthcare rights of women versus Catholic teaching is particularly important in the US, because about one in ten of American acute-care hospitals is Catholic sponsored or affiliated. Therefore women who do not agree with Catholic teaching do not always have access to a non-Catholic hospital. Critics have argued that this situation takes away women's right to a procedure that is available in other parts of the US. However, to Catholic personnel, the unborn child is as much a patient as the mother, so that they are not willing to kill one patient in order to save another.

The Bishops and the Press

The Catholic Bishops have been condemned by the US press for interfering in matters that do not concern them. However, the Bishops have a duty to teach the Catholic faith, which includes a duty to provide guidance on how that faith applies to daily life. Thus the Bishops are speaking the truth, as taught by the Catholic Church.

The lawsuit highlights the contrast between those who follow what the Church considers to be the objective truth and those who are guided by what seems right at the moment, that is, a subjective truth. In my view, the opposition between these two attitudes represents the fundamental moral conflict of our times, which can only deepen as Church teaching and secular legislation diverge.

In terms of official teaching, the Catholic Church stands almost alone in claiming the right to life of every human being from conception to natural death. However, the decisions about defending human life at its beginning and end rests largely with ordinary men and women, because they are the one's who make the choices about using IVF, having an abortion or seeking help to die. Catholics involved in health care also have to decide whether to take part in in these practices. The attitude of these two groups of ordinary people is therefore crucial for the protection of the most vulnerable human lives. We will consider the former group in the next chapter, but here we focus on the dilemmas of those who work in health care.

The Decisions of Health Care Personnel

As abortion is often the area of greatest controversy, I want to tell the story of two Catholic Scottish midwives who objected to being involved in abortion in any way. Connie Wood and Mary Doogan had been required to supervise staff carrying out abortions in the hospital where they worked. They refused to do so, citing the UK Abortion Act, which states that no one shall be 'under any duty ... to participate in any treatment authorised by this Act to which he has a conscientious objection.'[22] The midwives contended that this clause gave them the right to refuse to supervise personnel carrying out abortions.

As the hospital disagreed with them, they sought to have their rights acknowledged via the courts. Their case went to appeal and then to the Supreme Court. At every step the court decision hinged on the interpretation of the term *participate*. Did it refer solely to *direct participation* or did it include *indirect participation*, such as supervision of those carrying out an abortion?

In 2012 a court in Edinburgh ruled that the two women did not have the right to conscientious objection, because they were not required to be directly involved in abortions. However, the Court of Appeal reversed this ruling, stating that the right extended to the 'whole process of treatment', not just to the actual medical or surgical termination.

The health authority took the case to the Supreme Court which overturned the ruling of the Appeal Court, stating that, if managers had the right to conscientious objection, so might the caterers and cleaners serving the wards to which abortion patients were admitted, because all could be said to facilitate abortions in some way.[23]

The final ruling in this case places anyone involved with the many medical procedures that threaten human life today in a difficult position; they have to decide not only whether they can be directly involved, but also whether they can carry out tasks that constitute fairly remote co-operation. What does the Church say about such cases?

Co-operation in Wrong-doing

According to the Church, there are two different ways in which a person can participate or co-operate in a wrong action. They can carry out the action because they agree with it in principle, for example, they may believe it is acceptable to abort a child, or they can co-operate in someone else's wrong-doing, for instance by managing the roster for performing abortions. The Church calls the former action *formal co-operation in evil*, the latter *material co-operation in evil*.[24]

In the eyes of the Catholic Church, *formal co-operation* is never permissible. However, *material co-operation* raises much more complex questions. There are many levels of *material co-operation* and different people may reach different decisions about the extent to which they are willing to co-operate.

For instance, two people working in a pharmacy that sells the morning-after pill, which often causes early abortions, may reach different conclusions about the morality of working in such a business. One of them may decide that it is acceptable to work there, as the job mostly involves providing medication rather than abortifacients. However, another person may feel called to bear witness to their belief that abortion is morally wrong by seeking a different job.

Decisions about *material co-operation* are difficult to make, because circumstances vary so much from person to person. Therefore each individual needs to get as much information about the situation as possible and consider the consequences of their decision, before carrying it out.

Truth and the Protection of Human Life

When the UN drew up the *Universal Declaration of Human Rights*, it did not define what it meant by *everyone*. In particular, there was no common understanding of the rights of the embryo and unborn child. In practice, individual member states interpreted the right to life at these early stages as they wished, often legalising the destruction of human life before birth. Increasingly, people at the end of life are also at risk through various forms of euthanasia, so that the universal right to life is not universally observed.

The recognition of the right to life of all is therefore left mainly to religious teaching, above all the teaching of the Catholic Church. In his document *Peace on Earth* (*Pacem in Terris*), which, like the document by Pope St John Paul II referred to earlier, is addressed to everyone of good will, Pope St John XXIII has covered much of the same ground as the *Declaration.* However, he also goes beyond the areas dealt with in the UN document, reminding the reader that the foundation for all rights and duties is the fact that God has created everyone in his own image. This means that every human being is called to live in a way that is worthy of such a being, above all by respecting the lives of all, including one's own. The document states unequivocally that 'the right to live involves the duty to preserve one's life.'[25]

The attempts to take charge of life by assuming the right to destroy unborn or seriously ill human beings, is the result of the conflict between God and man which began with the Fall. If man accepts life as God-given, then all life must be respected. If, on the other hand, man begins to distinguish between lives that are worth living and lives that are not, then that has catastrophic consequences not only for the weakest members of society, but for everyone.

Conclusion

In our times there is a tendency to relegate religious belief to the private sphere. However, beliefs about the value of all human life have practical applications. As we have seen, Catholic hospitals have come into conflict with the law in some countries and Catholic bishops have been sued for upholding the teaching of the Church. All this is evidence of an irreconcilable difference between the teaching of the Catholic Church about human life and the legislation of most countries.

Catholic health care personnel (and non-Catholics who agree with them) are at the forefront of this conflict. They are faced with the stark choice between pulling out of all specialities which might require them to act against the teaching of the Church and continuing to bear witness to their faith, until they come to a disagreement with their employers that forces them to resign. In either case they will pay a heavy price for adhering to their beliefs.

In some situations, such as the Chilean mining disaster mentioned earlier, everyone, whatever their religion, nationality or origin, will understand that it is imperative to try to save life. However, in other circumstances, the need to save lives is less immediately obvious and here the Church and the state often differ. The Church believes every human being has the right to life, whereas the state increasingly permits the destruction of some human lives. As time goes on, this conflict is likely to deepen, thereby affecting ever-greater numbers of Catholic institutions and individuals.

Overall Summary

- The UN was founded in order to protect all human life, notably through the *Declaration of Human Rights*.

- Recent UN calls for a right to abortion contradicts its original aim of protecting human life.
- With a few notable exceptions, the legislation of individual states and countries no longer protects all human life before birth and when nearing its end.
- The Catholic Church stands almost alone in its claim that every human being has the right to life from conception to natural death.
- The teaching of the Catholic Church about the right to life of all, including the unborn child, has led to conflicts between Catholic-run hospitals and the civil authorities.
- Conflicts between Church and civil authorities, especially about abortion and euthanasia, are likely to increase in the future.
- Catholics who work in health care are at the sharp end of the conflict about the right to life of all.

Catholic health care workers are most frequently affected by the clash between legislation and Catholic teaching, but other Catholics are also faced with difficult decisions about issues such as infertility, a problem pregnancy or extreme pain or handicap. In such cases many people seek to avoid suffering by destroying human life. Those who choose to respect all human life will almost certainly also accept suffering as a result of their choice. We will consider such situations in the next chapter.

Notes

[1]   http://www.un.org/en/sections/un-charter/preamble/index.html (10 October 2015).
[2]   Introductory words preceding the text of the Declaration as published on http://www.un.org/Overview/rights.html. (28 September 2005) and D. P. Forsythe, *Human Rights in International*

Relations, (Cambridge:Cambridge University Press, 2000), pp. 35–36.

3   *Universal   Declaration   of   Human   Rights*,   3, http://www.un.org/Overview/rights.html (28 September 2005).

4   *UN Convention on the Rights of the Child*, 1989, Preamble, http://www.hrweb.org/legal.child.html (30 September 2005).

5   *UN Convention on the Rights of the Child*, 1989, 6.1, http://www.hrweb.org/legal.child.html (30 September 2005).

6   *The Guardian*, 24 October 2011.

7   CNS News http://cnsnews.com/news/article/un-chief-calls-universal-access-abortion-and-contraception-teen-girls (5 June 2012).

8   *Universal   Declaration   of   Human   Rights*,   25.1, http://www.un.org/Overview/rights.html (28 September 2005).

9   Concluding observations of the *Human Rights Committee*: Netherlands. 27 August 2001, C. 'Principal Subjects of Concern and Recommendations', http://www.unhchr.ch/tbs/doc.nsf (1 March 2012).

10 Office of the United Nations High Commissioner for Human Rights, 'Human Rights, Terrorism and Counter-terrorism', Fact Sheet No. 32, Geneva 2008, 3.B 'What is terrorism?', http://www.ohchr.org/Documents/publications/Factsheet32EN .pdf (6 March 2012).

11 'Straight UN Facts', 'There is no UN definition of terrorism', http://www.eyeontheun.org/facts.asp?1=1&p=61 (6 March 2012).

12 La. Rev. Stat. Ann. para.9:126, as quoted *in National Conference of State Legislatures*, 'Embryo and Gamete Disposition Laws', http://www.ncsl.org/issues-research/health/embryo-and-gamete-disposition-laws.aspx (13 March 2012).

13 K. A. Moore, 'Embryo Adoption: The Legal and Moral Challenges', http://www.faculty.law.miami.edu/mcoombs/documents /Moore.EmbryoAdoption.doc , pp. 113–115.(3 June 2007)

14 UN website on population, http://www.un.org/esa/population /publications/abortion/doc/ , then go to 'Ireland'. (28 May 2011).

15 As reported by *Human Rights Watch*, 16 December 2010, http://www.hrw.org/en/news/2010/12/16/ireland-european-court/ (21 July 2011).

16 'Library   of   Congress   http://www.loc.gov/law/foreign-news/article/ireland-government-response-to-loss-in-european-court-ruling-on-abortion-law/ (15 October 2015) and S.Lynch,

'Council of Europe Closes Case against Ireland on Abortion', *The Irish Times*, 4 December 2014.

17   Pope John Paul II, *Evangelium Vitae*, Heading.

18   Pope John Paul II, *Evangelium Vitae*, 4.

19   http://www.loc.gov/law/foreign-news/article/ireland-government-response-to-loss-in-european-court-ruling-on-abortion-law/,http://www.irishtimes.com/news/social-affairs/mater-hospital-to-comply-with-legislation-1.1539781 and http://www.catholicherald.co.uk/news/2013/10/03/mater-hospital-will-not-perform-abortions-says-board-member/ (21 October 2015).

20   *The Irish Catholic*, 14 May 2015.

21   *American Civil Liberties Union*, 'Tamesha Means v. United States Conference of Catholic Bishops', https://www.aclu.org/print/node/3704 (30 June 2015).

22   UK Abortion Act 1967, Section 4(1).

23   BBC News 17 December 2014, http://www.bbc.co.uk/news/uk-scotland-glasgow-west.-30514054 (2 November 2015).

24   Catholic Bishops' Conference of England and Wales, *Cherishing Life*, (London: Catholic Truth Society and Colloquium (CaTEW),2004), 46,47.

25   Pope John XXIII, *Pacem in Terris*, 3,29.

8 SUFFERING AND A GOOD LIFE

ANY PEOPLE BELIEVE that a good life does not involve suffering. They also believe that life is not worth living, if suffering cannot be removed or alleviated. However, this is not how everyone reacts.

There are stories of great courage in the face of unavoidable suffering, which prove that a sufferer can indeed have a good life. The account of Stephen Sutton's short life is one of the most striking of these.

Stephen was diagnosed with incurable cancer at the age of fifteen. Instead of giving up on life, he decided that he would make the most of whatever time he had left. He began by making a long list of all the things he wanted to achieve before he died. Initially, it was his main aim to carry out as many of the items on the list as possible, but as time went by, he began to focus on helping others and this became his priority. He started fundraising for a charity called *Teenage Cancer Trust*, originally with the aim of raising £1 million; in the event, he raised over £5 million to help set up teenage cancer centres in NHS hospitals in the UK.

This brave young man died in 2014, aged only twenty, but in his short life he had truly become a 'neighbour' to his fellow cancer sufferers. He did not dwell on his own suffering, but sought to help others instead.[1] He had indeed achieved a good life.

Stephen's response to his diagnosis is the exact opposite of the reaction of the Dutch girl described in an earlier chapter. This girl was also seriously ill, but instead of trying to do something for others while she could, she sought to squeeze as much pleasure for herself out of her last days as possible; she then went through with the euthanasia she had been granted by the Dutch health care authorities.

The reactions of these two young people to their terminal illnesses reveal two fundamentally different attitudes to suffering. One decided to accept the disease, while doing the best he could with the life he had been given, while the other sought to avoid her illness by having herself killed.

There are many different circumstances in which suffering cannot be removed and which present the sufferer with a choice between living with the pain and making something of life—and eliminating it by destroying life.

It is important to bear in mind that suffering is not necessarily caused only by illness. It can be caused, for instance, by the news that an unborn child is seriously handicapped or by an inability to conceive. Let us look at some situations which present the sufferer with a life-and-death choice.

Suffering and Infertility

I once spoke with an elderly lady whose daughter had just had a baby. 'It was wonderful', the lady said, 'my daughter had tried so hard to conceive and it was her fourth attempt at IVF when she managed to get pregnant and now she and her husband have a little girl.' Of course it was wonderful—and yet—what about the embryos that would inevitably have been destroyed by using IVF?

I tried, as tactfully as possible, to indicate that there were problems with this method, but the grandmother simply said, 'Oh, well, there was, of course, some defective material that couldn't be used.' This is indeed how many people see the embryo destruction associated with this method of conceiving. However, once a couple have understood that the embryo is a human being, they may well feel that they cannot use IVF; this was the painful conclusion reached by another couple I came across.

When this couple found they were unable to have children, they decided they could not try to conceive via IVF. 'It was a hard decision for us,' the husband said, 'but we were not prepared to destroy the potential brothers and sisters of any child we might have.' Even if it were to become practical to implant all the embryos created, so that IVF would not entail the loss of embryonic life, the method would still not be acceptable to the Catholic Church, because it involves a separation of conception from the act of love.[2]

Suffering and the Unborn Child

Handicapped Child

When a pregnant woman discovers that she is expecting a handicapped child, it is common for her decide to have an abortion. Following the pre-natal diagnosis of Down's syndrome, for instance, the majority of children are aborted, though a small percentage of parents decide to carry on with the pregnancy. In 2010, of the 1,188 babies diagnosed with Down's syndrome in the UK, at least 80% were aborted. Of the rest, many were stillborn or the mother miscarried, so that only 3% were born alive.

By respecting the child's right to life, this small group of parents also accepted the suffering, as well as the joy, associated with bringing up their child.[3] I have seen how lovingly some parents care for a child with this disability and how much that child can be part of the family.

Risk to the Mother's Life

When the expected child is considered to pose a risk to the mother's life or health, many women are advised to have an abortion, thereby placing their own life before that of their child. In 1962 the Italian doctor, Gianna Molla, found herself in precisely this situation. While pregnant with her fourth child, she discovered that she had a cancerous growth on her womb. She was told that the two safest procedures for her were either to cut out the entire womb with the baby inside, or to remove the growth, while carrying out an abortion at the same time. The latter option would leave her the possibility of having more children later.

The least safe option, from Gianna's point of view, was to have the growth removed while leaving the baby in the womb. This was because the stitches left after the operation might burst as the child grew, posing a risk to the mother's life. However, as this was the only way of giving the child a chance to survive, she decided to choose this option. She told her parish priest that she was ready for anything, for any suffering, as long as she could save her baby.[4]

The operation went well and she was able to carry on with the pregnancy, but, as a doctor, she was well aware that complications associated with the birth might put her own life at risk.

In due course, Gianna had a healthy baby girl by caesarean section, but the path she had chosen turned out to be costly for her. She survived for long enough to see the child and to know that her baby was safe, but then peritonitis set in and she died after a week. The child she had born later became a doctor like her mother.

Many people would say that, in a case like this, there were good reasons for sacrificing the expected child for the sake not only of the mother, but of the husband and the other children. However, Gianna felt that she must at least give her fourth child a chance of survival, even if it meant great suffering for herself and her family. It was evident to those around the family that both her husband, and, later on, her children accepted and supported her decision. Her husband lived to be present when the Church declared Gianna a saint in 2004.

Suffering and Disability

The situation of an incurably ill or disabled person who wants to die is completely different to the cases of the embryo and the unborn child that we have just considered. The sick or disabled person does not kill somebody else, but seeks help to kill him or herself. In the following examples two sufferers give totally different responses to this problem.

The Spanish-teacher Marini McNeilly, who had originally come from the Basque Country, was left almost totally paralysed after a stroke, with only a little movement in her head and face. Suddenly, she could no longer communicate with other people, let alone teach.

After two years' treatment, Marini could move her head more and had also regained some movement in her fingers. She was able to hold a conversation by selecting letters on an alphabet board and to use a computer by means of her eye movements.

This is the kind of situation in which some people have asked to be helped to die. In an interview a few years ago, she was asked about a man in similar circumstances to hers, who had appealed through the courts for access to euthanasia.[5] She slowly spelled out the words,

> Hope is the last thing you should lose. ...
>
> Where there is a challenge there is hope to meet it.[6]

In the course of the interview she said that the people who cared about her, especially her husband, had given her the strength of will to go on living and to keep trying to improve her situation. Clearly she did not feel that the extreme suffering of her disabilities was a reason to give up on life. When asked how she felt now, she replied, 'Full of optimism.'

The *Times* columnist, Melanie Reid, and Marini McNeilly have much in common. Melanie Reid was paralysed in a riding accident, leaving her unable to walk and with only limited movement in her arms and hands. In her weekly column, she writes about her slow recovery, the setbacks and her determination to live and make the most of life in spite of her disabilities.

Nevertheless, in 2012, she wrote an article in support of assisted suicide and euthanasia. She advocated the right of people who felt their lives had become intolerable to be given help to die, stating that this right was 'the most basic human right of all'. At the same time, she said,

> I choose, fiercely, to live for the people who love me; and will continue to do so until such point as they understand I cannot carry on.[7]

Both in the interview with Marini McNeilly and in the writing of Melanie Reid there is a strong sense that life can be good in spite of suffering and also a sense of obligation to go on living for the sake of the people who love them. Yet Melanie claims the right to assisted suicide as an insurance policy against unbearable suffering.

In these two different attitudes we see the contrast between a willingness to accept life and make the most of it, however hard it may be, and a conditional acceptance that holds on to a right to death as an ultimate means of control.

Suffering due to Social Conditions

Health problems are not the only cause of suffering; many people live under a repressive regime or a government whose aims they disagree with and we have considered examples of the suffering this can cause in an earlier chapter. In rare cases extremists turn to violence and even the taking of human life in order to change the society they live in or as an act of revenge against perceived enemies. The 9/11 and 7/7 attacks in New York and London are examples of this.

As a counterpoint to such attacks, I want to describe someone who has opposed an oppressive regime without resorting to violence of any kind.

The Burmese campaigner for democracy Aung San Suu Kyi was kept under house arrest for some sixteen years by the ruling military dictatorship in her country. From behind the gates of her compound she remained a powerful symbol of the fight for political rights in her country.

While she was under house arrest, she was sometimes permitted visits from her family and from political supporters, but she was not allowed a last visit from her British husband, after he was diagnosed with terminal cancer; nor could she go to visit him, because the ruling junta would not have allowed her to return to her country.

In spite of this great personal sacrifice, she did not resort even to violent language, but remained courteous and dignified in her opposition to the military regime. In 2010 she was finally released from house arrest and won a seat in parliament, after elections were permitted in 2012. In the most recent of these, in 2015, she won a majority of the votes.

Aung San Suu Kyi's way of dealing with the treatment imposed on her by the dictatorship could be called 'the way of patience'. Rather than inflicting suffering on others

through violence, she bore the hardships of her imprisonment without complaint. At the same time she continued
to oppose the regime by peaceful means both through her
writings and through speeches to her supporters, when
these were allowed.[8] Since her release from house arrest
and re-entry into politics, Suu Kyi has been heavily
criticised for not speaking out against her government's
brutal treatment of the Rohingyas. Nevertheless, her
attitude while in prison remains a valid example of personal restraint.

What Price a Good Life?

In each of the situations we have discussed above, those
involved had to determine at what price they were willing
to achieve a good life. Above all, they had to decide whether
it was ever right to seek this by taking a human life.

   We have considered these topics many times, because
they are fundamental to understanding what constitutes a
good life. If it is a life without suffering, then there might be
a case for a right to die or even to kill defective or unwanted
human beings. If, on the other hand, a good life is a life lived
in truth, then everyone can have a good life, because then
such a life can include suffering. Indeed, it might be necessary to accept suffering in order to lead a good life. This was
the case, for instance, with the childless couple who decided
not to use IVF and for the Basque teacher who decided to
go on living, despite her severe handicaps.

Subjective versus Objective Truth

In Western society, the right to life of every innocent
human being has long been considered an objective truth,
that is, it is true in itself, and its inclusion in the *Declaration of Human Rights* shows how widely it is accepted.

However, this objective truth has now come into conflict with a number of subjective truths which can be summarised under the heading of a right to take a human life or lives that get in the way of my good life. We see this, for instance, in the clamour for a universal right to abortion and in the ongoing debate about a right to assisted suicide and euthanasia. Arguments in favour particularly of the latter are often based on a desire to show compassion for those who suffer, but is it really compassion?

Compassion and Suffering

Compassion means feeling for and suffering with the suffering person. There are many ways of showing compassion, such as the many acts of kindness that we are all capable of. Above all, it means seeing the suffering person through the eyes of the Samaritan who took care of the man left for dead by the roadside and did all he could for him.

Nevertheless, some people today would see it as a kindness to put an end to someone's pain by helping them to die. However, the way in which we show compassion for somebody needs to be guided by our duty to respect every human life. It needs to be guided by the truth.

If we fail to protect those who are handicapped or suffering from disease, or simply unwanted, we, as a society, are led down a slippery slope towards a general assumption that only healthy, able-bodied people are worth keeping alive. We have already seen this at its worst in Nazi Germany, where adults and young people suffering from physical or mental handicap were systematically killed.

Many people believe that the destruction of human beings at the beginning and end of life that takes place today is completely different, because it is motivated by compassion and, at the end of life, mostly voluntary on the part of the person who is helped to die. However, it is only a small step from taking such lives for compassionate reasons, to thinking that a life with handicap is not worth living, to believing that handicapped people are worthless and can therefore be disposed of. This is compassion gone wrong.

Compassion Gone Wrong

John Wyndham's classic science-fiction story *Compassion Circuit* illustrates poignantly the way in which compassion can go wrong. Wyndham describes a future world in which sophisticated robots do much of the humdrum work that humans used to do. In this world, most couples have a 'domestic robot' to do all the housework, but Janet, the main character of the story, feels uneasy at the thought of being left alone all day with a robot, while George, her husband, is at work. (The story was first published in 1956, hence the tacit assumption that a married woman was likely to be a housewife).

Janet suffers from a debilitating disease and eventually becomes so run-down that she has to go into hospital for treatment. In hospital, Janet is cared for by a sympathetic nurse, who turns out to be a robot. This fact persuades Janet that it would be good for her to have her own robot at home. Janet gets the very latest robot whose special feature is a built-in 'compassion circuit'. This feature will enable the robot to look after Janet better than any other model, or so it is thought. The 'compassion-protection circuit' works by evaluating every order and obeying only those it considers harmless to the owner.[9]

As soon as Janet is out of hospital, her domestic robot arrives and she begins to tell it all her troubles, as if it were indeed human and this is where the trouble begins. Janet keeps saying that she wishes she was strong like the robot.

Her complaints activate the robot's compassion circuit, so that it tells her, that, 'if anything goes wrong with us [robots] ... it doesn't hurt and is easily replaced.' It goes on to say that her pain 'disturbs my compassion-circuit.'[10]

The computer tells Janet that it is much better to replace the weak parts of a system, before it totally breaks down. From then on, the compassion circuit takes over the lives of Janet and George, like Fate in a Greek tragedy.

The robot persuades Janet to go back to hospital, so that she can become the strong, healthy woman she wants to be for her husband. She even accepts what is referred to as the 'ultimate' treatment. George is then called to the hospital, where he is told that his wife has already agreed to the treatment that is best for her. The hospital robot warns him that otherwise death will be the inevitable outcome.[11] Not fully understanding what is at stake, but wishing to do all he can for his wife, George signs the consent form, so that Janet's treatment can go ahead.

After some days, during which he is not allowed to see his wife, George gets home to find that Janet has returned from hospital and is in bed with only her head visible. He begins to sense that something is wrong, when she says that she 'didn't really mean to do it' and 'didn't fully understand what was going to happen'. Concerned, George takes his wife's hand, only to find it is dreadfully cold, as cold as ... He flings back the bedclothes—to find, not Janet, but the body of a robot.

Rushing out of the room in blind despair, he stumbles and falls down the stairs, breaking his back and legs. The domestic robot calmly picks him up, assesses the damage and, moved by its compassion circuit, calls for an ambulance. It explains that the man would be crippled for life, even if he did get over his injuries. Much better to give him the same treatment as his wife and, as for the form,

... that'll be quite all right. His wife will sign it.[12]

Why does this story have such power to shock? Because the reader immediately realises that the robot had failed to grasp the essential truth that Janet is a living human being, not a piece of machinery. We ignore this truth at our cost, when we treat sick or handicapped people as malfunctioning bits of machinery that should be discarded, if they cannot be repaired.

Suffering in a Christian Context

The robot could not understand the difference between a person and a machine, but we do have that capacity. However, it may take a moment of truth for us to begin to see particular groups of people as fully human.

For instance, for American slave owners of the early nineteenth century, the realisation that it was inherently wrong to own some of their fellow-human beings might have come as a shock. Nevertheless, once they had understood this truth and accepted it, they might feel obliged to set their slaves free. This, in turn, might lead to financial ruin and the suffering that went with it, but that would be the price of living by the truth.

In a similar way, the realisation that every human being from conception to natural death has the right to life brings with it an obligation to respect all human life. This may mean, for instance, accepting childlessness, an unwanted pregnancy or the suffering of a serious disease— if the only way out of these would involve the destruction of human life.

Christ's Life as the Perfect Model of a Good Life

Christ's life is the perfect model of a good life, a model offered not only to Christians, but to everyone. This does not mean that those who follow Christ are called to make their lives an exact copy of his life, but that they are called to live as Christ would have done, in their circumstances and in their time. However, like Christ, they must live by the truth, regardless of the suffering and difficulties involved.

Christ bore witness to the truth in all his actions, but above all in his encounter with Pilate, the Roman Governor of Palestine. The account in the Gospel of St John focuses on two fundamentally different attitudes to truth: Christ stands before Pilate as Truth Incarnate; Pilate, on the other hand, has an ambivalent attitude. He is aware that the man before him is innocent, but disregards this fact, when he is warned that he will be disloyal to the Emperor, if he lets Jesus go free.

I will explain some of the background to the scene between Jesus and Pilate and then describe their encounter in some detail, as it is central to an understanding of what it means to follow the truth, regardless of the cost.

At the time of Jesus, Palestine was under Roman domination, but with a measure of self-government. However, the Jewish authorities did not have the right to put a man to death, and since they wanted to condemn Christ to death, they had to bring him before the Roman Governor. The main charge against Jesus, from the point of view of the Jewish authorities, was that Jesus had claimed to be the Son of God, which, in their eyes, was a blasphemy deserving death.

However, in order to ensure that Pilate would pronounce the death sentence, they emphasised that Jesus had described himself as a king, and hence a potential threat to the Roman Emperor.[13]

Pilate therefore feels that he must put Jesus on trial and he begins by asking him whether he really claims to be a king:

To which Jesus replies,

> Mine is not a kingdom of this world. If my kingdom
> were of this world, my men would have fought to
> prevent my being surrendered to the Jews. As it is,
> my kingdom does not belong here.[14]

Pilate asks,

> So, then you are a king?[15]

Christ answers,

> I am a king. I was born for this, ... to bear witness
> to the truth; and all who are on the side of truth
> listen to my voice.[16]

Pilate now realises that his interrogation is leading towards
a question he is not willing to face. So he scoffs,

> 'Truth, what is that?'[17]

The Roman Governor does not wish to engage with the
deeper meaning of truth; he does, however, believe in truth
as understood in a court of law and therefore announces
to the Jews assembled outside,

> I find no case against him...[18]

Then the Jews bring forward their main charge against
Jesus,

> We have a law, and according to that law he ought
> to be put to death, because he has claimed to be
> the Son of God.[19]

'The Son of God!' Pilate is now afraid both of the consequences of crucifying this enigmatic figure and of angering
the mob before him by not doing so. Playing for time, he
asks Christ where he comes from, meaning, 'who are you,
really?', but Christ does not answer.[20]

Then Pilate says,

Are you refusing to speak to me? Surely you know
I have power to release you and I have power to
crucify you?[21]

To which Christ makes the disturbing reply,

You would have no power over me at all if it had
not been given you from above.[22]

Pilate is by now terrified of harming this man who seems
to exist in a world beyond his comprehension. However,
Pilate also fears the Emperor's wrath, if he lets a potential
rebel go free. The Jews produce the argument that makes
his mind up for him,

If you set him free you are no friend of Caesar's;
anyone who makes himself king is defying Caesar.[23]

Pilate then reveals what is really important to him, which
is neither religious truth nor legal truth, but his own
advantage. He therefore decides to have the man crucified,
even though he knows that Jesus is innocent and that his
kingdom is not a threat to the Emperor.

Choosing the Truth

Both Jesus and Pilate are faced with a fundamental choice:
They can seek to extricate themselves from a dangerous
situation by disregarding the truth or they can be faithful
to the truth and accept the suffering that will follow.

Pilate's had to choose between accepting the fact that
Christ was innocent and ignoring it in order to appear in
a good light before the Emperor; Pilate chose the latter.

Christ also had a choice: He could have decided to use
his power as the Son of God to overcome those who sought
to arrest him and have him killed. ('My men would have
fought to prevent my being surrendered ...') However, he
would then have contradicted the very nature of his

kingdom, which is based on truth, not power. Christ therefore let the truth speak for itself and, in so doing, accepted the suffering inflicted by his enemies.

The need to choose between truth and falsehood that is described so poignantly in the scene between Christ and Pilate occurs again and again in all our lives, even if in less dramatic circumstances.

For ordinary people today, most of the situations in which living in truth becomes costly concern respect for the right to life of very vulnerable human beings. The choice here is usually between taking human life, in order to avoid suffering, and protecting life, while accepting the suffering that will be the consequence.

Conscience: the Sense for Recognising the Truth

How does anyone discover the truth? Pope Emeritus Benedict has strikingly spoken of the human conscience as the sense for recognising the truth; our consciences therefore work rather like our other senses, such as seeing and hearing. The Pope refers to a passage in which St Paul states that the conscience 'bears witness' in the hearts of everyone, including his pagan contemporaries.[24]

Regardless of our religious beliefs, we can all discover that the right to life belongs to everyone; Christians will add that the still, small voice of conscience comes from God, to guide them towards the truth.

In a perfect world this would mean that the promptings of conscience would always lead everyone to the truth and enable them to live by it. However, in a world affected by sin, it is not always easy to distinguish clearly between right and wrong, so that people sometimes make choices that do not agree with the truth. We have seen the catastrophic effects of such decisions, especially in relation to the deliberate destruction of so many embryos and unborn children in our times. The protection of human life requires an unfailing openness to the truth, so as to live by it, whatever the cost.

Suffering and the Kingdom of God

There is something in all of us which cries out against suffering and which instinctively understands not only that it is right to alleviate it, but that there must be a way of life that is both good and free of suffering.

Christ's healing ministry justifies this gut feeling, because when John the Baptist, the last prophet before Christ, sent messengers to ask if Jesus was the Messiah, Jesus pointed to the many sick and disabled people who were cured,

> ... the blind see again, the lame walk, those suffering from virulent skin-diseases are cleansed ...[25]

These cures were a sign that the Kingdom of God was now at work in the world and that Christ was indeed the Messiah, who had come to usher in a new era in world history.

Why, then, is there still suffering in the world? Why has everyone in need not been healed? These questions have troubled people down the ages and will go on doing so. Here it is only possible to attempt an answer in connection with the healings as signs of the Kingdom. They showed that the Kingdom was at work in the world, but they were only a foretaste of how things would be after it had finally broken through, at the Second Coming of Christ.

In the present age, we are living in the in-between time between the First and the Second Comings of Christ. During that time, we experience all the hardships and illnesses that came into the world after the Fall. Our response must not be to remove them by destroying human life, but to do everything possible to cure diseases and make life better for those who suffers in any way. In so doing, we will follow the example of Christ, who lived in truth, while accepting the suffering and death it cost him. However, the effects of the Fall will not last forever.

The Second Coming

After the Second Coming, there will be no more suffering, but it will have left its marks on Christ and all who have lived according to his will, whether they knew him or not.

We can see this from the fact that, when Christ appeared to his disciples after his Resurrection, he showed them his hands and his side, which still bore the marks of the crucifixion. That was the occasion when he invited Thomas to touch the wound in his side and to look at the nail-marks in his hands and to believe that he had indeed risen from the dead.[26]

Using symbolic language, the Book of Revelation speaks of Christ in Heaven as a Lamb that bears the marks of having been sacrificed. Christ will show the signs of his suffering for all time and so will his followers.[27] They will not continue to feel pain, any more than Christ will continue to feel pain, but their suffering, like that of Christ, will bear fruit in eternity and therefore have a permanent place in the good life of Heaven.

Conclusion: Working for the Breakthrough of the Kingdom

Does the fact that suffering must be accepted as part of life during the present phase of the world's history mean that it should not be alleviated? Are Christians simply required to wait patiently for death and the Second

Coming of Christ and, in the meantime, put up with whatever hardship comes their way? There has certainly been a tendency among some Christians to think so, especially in the past.

However, that is not how they, or anyone else, are meant to behave in the face of suffering. On the contrary, the alleviation of suffering by means that respect human life is very much part of the Christian life. The many religious orders dedicated to caring for the sick are only one example of this.

Christ's call to his followers to proclaim the Kingdom implies a call to work for that Kingdom, in practical terms too. During the solemn liturgy of Good Friday, the day on which Christ died for the whole world, the Catholic Church prays for everyone in that world; it prays for those within the Church and those outside it and, in particular, it asks for God's help for all those who suffer in any way. The prayers implore God to 'banish disease' and grant 'health to the sick'.[28]

Such prayers imply a readiness to take an active part in alleviating suffering, wherever this is possible. It means that Church members must be willing to be God's hands and feet, in whatever ways he wants to use them.

It is not only Christians who are called to alleviate suffering. I do not know if Stephen, the young cancer sufferer, was a believer, but his life was certainly a remarkable example of neighbourly love in action. A life such as his shows with great clarity that it is possible to have a good life, while accepting unavoidable suffering.

Overall Summary

- A good life is always a life lived in truth.

- Conscience is the organ which enables people to recognise the truth.
- Every effort should be made to alleviate suffering, while respecting the right to life of everyone.
- Christ bore witness to the truth, knowing that this would lead to suffering.
- Pilate avoided the truth in order to avoid suffering.
- The healings of Christ were the initial signs of the breakthrough of the Kingdom.
- After the Second Coming of Christ, there will be no more suffering.
- The marks of suffering will remain with Christ and his followers as signs of their fidelity to the truth.

The means by which people seek to relieve suffering depend on whether they respect all human life or whether they believe they have the right to destroy some lives. In the final chapter we will show that the decision to respect all human life is the only basis for creating a society that includes everyone.

Notes

1   http://stephensstory.co.uk/ (11 November 2015).
2   See *Catechism of the Catholic Church*, 2377.
3   The remaining approximate figure of 17% is accounted for by still births, miscarriages and unknown outcomes. See *National Down's Syndrome Cytogenics Register*, 2010, www.wolfson.qmul .ac.uk/ndscr/reports/ (23 April 2012).
4   J. O. Maynard, *Gianna Molla* (London: Catholic Truth Society, 2000), p. 63.
5   *The Times*, 20 July 2010.
6   Interview in *The Times*, 24 July 2010.
7   *The Times*, 27 March 2012.
8   http://www.nobelprize.org/nobel_prizes/peace/laureates/1991

and http://www.bbc.co.uk/news/world-asia-pacific11685977? print=true (19 April 2012).

9   J. Wyndham, 'Compassion Circuit', *in The Seeds of Time*, (Harmondsworth:Penguin, 1983), p. 201.

10   Wyndham, 'Compassion Circuit', p. 206.

11   *Ibid.*, p. 209.

12   *Ibid.*, p. 211.

13   Lk 23:2–5.

14   Jn 18:36–37.

15   Jn 18:37a.

16   Jn 18:37b.

17   Jn 18:37b.

18   Jn 18:39.

19   Jn 19:7b.

20   Jn 19:9 and Note b, *The New Jerusalem Bible* (London: Darton, Longman & Todd, 1985).

21   Jn 19:10.

22   Jn 19:11.

23   Jn 19:12.

24   J. Cardinal Ratzinger, *Truth and Tolerance, Christian Belief and World Religions*, (San Francisco: Ignatius Press, 2004), p. 205f. The reference to St. Paul is to Rm 2:14–15.

25   Lk 7:22.

26   Jn 20:27.

27   Rev 5:9,12; 6:9; 7:14; 14:13.

28   'General Intercessions for Good Friday', X, *The CTS New Sunday Missal* (London: Catholic Truth Society, 2011), p. 302.

9 TOWARDS A TRULY INCLUSIVE SOCIETY

In one of the parishes I have been in, there was a man with serious learning difficulties among the servers at mass. Let us call him John. One of the other servers was always at hand to help him, but it was obvious that he knew exactly what was going on and he faithfully attended, Sunday after Sunday, year after year. John's public role showed all of us in the congregation that he was not just a man with a handicap, but he was someone who could do something. He was valued and appreciated; but more than that, his unfailing service was a witness to everyone of fidelity to the Church, a very necessary witness, especially in today's world.

Yet John could easily have been among the many unborn children with a handicap, who are aborted all over the world. If John had been created for IVF and his handicap had been identified, he might have been killed at that stage. If he had been knocked down in the street and been left in a PVS state, those in charge of his care might have argued that he was not worth keeping alive. However, John's witness in the congregation was living proof that every human being has value and that every human life must be respected.

Christians believe that, at the end of life, we will have to give an account of how we have lived and the decisions we have made. In this chapter we will show that our basic attitudes to human life are crucial not only to how society will develop, but for our own ultimate fate.

A Good Life in the Future—Exclusion of some or Inclusion of All?

The search for a good life is closely bound up with beliefs about the right to life. There are two different paths: one respects only some human lives, whilst the other respects all human life.

Selective Respect for Human Life

Selective respect for life means that only some lives are protected, whereas others are considered expendable. This was the attitude of the eugenics movement in the late nineteenth and early twentieth centuries and it emerged in its most abhorrent form in the treatment of the sick and handicapped in Nazi Germany.

In our own times, a new form of selective respect is creeping in. We have seen this in the destruction of unwanted or handicapped embryos and unborn children and in the demand by some sick and disabled people for help to die, because they think their lives are not worth living. Many people interpret these developments as signs that the human race is finally taking charge of its destiny by ensuring that only those who can lead a worthwhile life remain alive. In such a society, a good life is a healthy and relatively pain-free life. The idea of life, all life, as a gift from God is receding into the background.

However, in the future, control may shift from the individual to some higher authority such as the state or a medical board. If the idea of a society in which various forms of mercy killing are imposed seems far-fetched, we have only to look at some of the practices that already exist or are seriously suggested. For instance, in China, those who broke the one-child policy that was in effect till recently have had a second child forcibly aborted.[1] There is evidence that some elderly people in the Netherlands are euthanised against their will. A respected contemporary philosopher has put forward the idea of a duty to die, once a person has reached a certain degree of dependency. All of these instances are signs of a loss of hope, of despair.

A Society Built on Despair

It is easy to imagine how the acceptance of mercy-killing for people whose quality of life is deemed insufficient could be widened to include the extermination of people who are thought to be inadequate in other respects. What about people with the wrong religion, the wrong opinions or those who are thought to be too morally deficient to make a positive contribution to society?

The fate of the latter is the subject of Hector Macdonald's chilling novel, *The Hummingbird Saint*, in which the S*aint*, (the leader of a commune in South America) seeks to create a community consisting solely of good and altruistic people. However, he himself sets the standard for such behaviour and anyone who, in his view, falls short of the mark is invited, or rather forced, to commit suicide.

The *Saint* also seeks to support good and altruistic people in the world at large, by giving them grants for charitable purposes. However, in order to qualify, applicants must spend some time in the commune in order to prove their worthiness. Only too late do they realise that, if they fail the goodness test, they will not leave the commune alive. The *Saint* wishes to cleanse not only his own commune, but the world at large of the morally deficient.

For such individuals there is no question of growth or healing, only the invitation to put an end to their existence. When seeking to justify the enforced suicide to a failed applicant, the *Saint* tells the unfortunate man that he is doing 'a good and brave thing' by removing himself from the world.[2]

However, at the end of the book, the commune leader realises the futility of his experiment. In order to comply with his own rules, he therefore decides to commit suicide. The book leaves it open whether he will go through with the suicide, but, significantly, his final words to one of his applicants are, 'God bless you'. To me, this is an indication that he is beginning to understand that a human being cannot put himself in God's place without doing terrible harm in the process. The *Saint's* only means of creating a good life was to destroy life, so that the society he had sought to create was built on despair.

A Society Built on Hope

Hope is the opposite of despair. A person who hopes looks to the future with confidence and expects something good, however difficult present circumstances might be. Marini McNeilly, the Basque woman who was almost totally paralysed after a stroke, said that hope was the last thing you should lose and she spoke of being full of optimism about her own future.

Hope protects the future of every human life, whereas despair cuts off the future, as was the case with the Dutch girl who ended her life so as to avoid becoming crippled by her degenerative disease.

The *Declaration of Human Rights* claims the right to life of every human being. It therefore looks to the future with hope. In the words of one author, it is

> the essential document, the touchstone, the creed
> of humanity that surely sums up all other creeds
> directing human behaviour.[3]

This is a 'creed' that everyone, regardless of religious persuasion, can subscribe to. The Bishops of England and

Wales have described the *Declaration* as representing a tradition that is very close to the 'spirit of the Gospel'.[4]

The 'spirit of the Gospel' is the compassionate spirit in which we saw the Samaritan care for the man who had been attacked by robbers. The Samaritan did not know this man; he was simply a 'neighbour' whose needs he could not overlook. In so doing, he gave the man hope.

Christian Hope

In his document, *On Christian Hope, (Spe Salvi)*, Pope Emeritus Benedict has spoken about the power of hope in every human life. Hope implies an attitude of trust in all that is good and, for believers, in God. Those who base their lives on hope seek to overcome as much suffering as possible by healing the sick, controlling pain and comforting those in distress; but they do not seek to avoid suffering at any cost.[5]

Pope Benedict describes a society that is unable to accept people who suffer as 'a cruel and inhuman society.'[6] This is because it throws away the sufferer with the suffering, so that the sufferer becomes a reject. Many people in contemporary Western society subscribe to this attitude, including the patients themselves. When sick or handicapped persons ask for help to die, a rejection of themselves can be part of their motivation.

However, according to the Pope Emeritus, it is precisely the ability to find meaning in their own pain that enables people to support others who suffer.[7] The inability and, sometimes, unwillingness, to accept suffering is at the root of many contemporary demands for embryo destruction and abortion as well as for assisted suicide and euthanasia. The belief that a good life must also be a comfortable and pain-free life is the main obstacle to a truly good life.

On the other hand, the acceptance of the right to life of every human being, however difficult the circumstances of that person, is a sign of hope. On a basis of hope, it is possible to support all who suffer in ways that respect their humanity. In what follows, we will look at some practical initiatives aimed at preserving life and therefore also hope for the future of everyone.

Hope for the Embryo

The question of how to treat the thousands of human embryos in cold storage is one of the most important moral problems of our times. According to Catholic belief, the embryo is a human being from the moment of conception, but unless he or she is implanted in a woman's womb, the embryo cannot grow to maturity and usually ends up being destroyed. The stored embryo is like a human person imprisoned in ice.

The Church has therefore called for an immediate halt to all production of embryos *in vitro*, but, even if this were to happen, it would not address the problem of the thousands of embryos already created and abandoned in fertility clinics.[8]

In such circumstances, it is not surprising that some people have tried to help the embryos escape from their frozen prison. One way of doing this is for a couple to donate their spare embryos to another couple, who then adopt the child. Clinics now also sometimes give unwanted embryos to infertile couples wishing to adopt them. One woman who had helped to rescue a frozen embryo in this way, said that embryos were children, 'just earlier.'[9]

The Catholic Church calls the motivation for embryo adoption 'praiseworthy'. Nevertheless, there are problems with such an adoption, because it breaks the link between the act of love and conception.[10] Current Church teaching has referred to the creation of embryos for whom there is no possibility of further development as a 'situation of injustice' for which there is no satisfactory resolution. [11]

However, if the sole motivation for adopting an embryo was to rescue an abandoned human being, I believe there might be a case for the Church to allow this; it could then be seen as comparable to the adoption of a child already born.

Such adoptions would help a few cases, but the only realistic hope for the embryo is to halt the practice of IVF, thereby ensuring that no human being is ever again conceived outside the mother's body. Hopefully the Church will have more to say about this difficult topic in the future.

Hope for the Unborn Child

The abortion of a child is an act of despair. It shows that those involved can think of no other way out of what is often a difficult situation. However, there are alternatives that do not involve the destruction of human life. For a woman in a crisis pregnancy, there are many organisations, often inspired by the Christian faith, that give support, for instance, with accommodation and finance.[12]

In the UK two of the main service providers are *LIFE* and *CareConfidential*.[13] In the US there is a large number of *Crisis Pregnancy Centers*, which will refer women for counselling and other support services, including the provision of baby clothes.[14]

A number of children are aborted because they are disabled. However, there are also examples of children with mental or physical disabilities being included in society. While not denying the difficulties of bringing up a disabled son or daughter, many people have spoken of the joy such a child has brought to the whole family.

In his recent document, *The Joy of Love* (*Amoris Laetitia*) Pope Francis has described handicapped children as 'a gift for the family'. He went on to say that the welcome given to such children was a test of everyone's commitment to include the most vulnerable in the community.[15]

In this connection, I would like to mention two long-standing initiatives aimed at ensuring that people with disabilities are treated as fellow-human beings. One of these seeks to include adults with learning difficulties in society, while the other helps children with a range of disabilities.

The *L'Arche* (The Ark) organisation was founded by the French Canadian Jean Vanier in 1964 with the intention of creating small communities where mentally disabled men and women could share a house with those of normal intelligence. In this way he hoped to point the way to the inclusion of people with learning disabilities in the more general community. *L'Arche* houses, which are based on the Christian faith, now exist throughout the world as a witness to the humanity of every individual, regardless of ability.

From a secular perspective, the UN set up UNICEF (the United Nation's Children's Fund) in 1946 to put into practice the ideals of its *Convention on the Rights of the Child*. UNICEF works for the inclusion of children with disabilities in society by giving them the same chances of education as other children.[16]

The testimony of individual families, as well as the work of organisations such as *L'Arche* and UNICEF, shows that despair need not be the reaction to the discovery that an expected child is disabled.[17]

Hope for Sick and Disabled People

Once a person has become severely disabled or seriously ill, there is a tendency today to regard their lives as not worth living. We have seen the rejection of such people both by those who care for them and by the sick or disabled themselves. These reactions stem from despair. If the value of the person is based on function only, then there is no hope for them, once that function has gone. Death can then appear to be the only way out.

However, the fact that people can no longer interact fully with their surroundings does not mean that they lose their value as human beings. If that value is recognised, then the life of the person must continue to command respect, both from the disabled themselves and from those who care for them. That is the basis, for instance, for the many initiatives in palliative care that have emerged today as a counter movement to Western demands for a right to die.

In the developing world, the work of Mother Teresa and her successors has been motivated by a desire to treat everyone, but especially the poorest and those close to death, with the compassion and respect they have a right to, simply as human beings.

The inspiration for Mother Teresa's work with the dying and destitute came, when she found a dying woman, half eaten by rats and ants, on a street in Calcutta. As the local hospital was reluctant to admit the woman, and as Mother Teresa now began to find more dying people on the streets, she asked for, and was given, a building where she could house them; this became her first *Home for the Dying Destitutes*. Her aim was to create an environment in which homeless people could meet kindness and love and feel that they, too, were children of God.[18]

In short, she treated them as neighbours, just as the Samaritan did when he found the wounded man by the roadside, while on his way from Jerusalem to Jericho.

Hope for those Tempted to Engage in Terrorism

Terrorist organisations often find willing supporters and recruits because of social conditions. It is therefore important that those in power do all they can to improve living conditions in the countries from which many terrorists originate.

In the short term, government aid can help reduce the risk of terrorism in the areas most affected. For instance, in Afghanistan, British aid has helped to establish an environment in which local businesses can develop. In the city of Herat in North-West Afghanistan, local furniture businesses are now employing some two hundred workers, both men and women. These are small beginnings, but, despite the continued threat from insurgents, they are positive signs in a country where one in three adults have cited unemployment as the main challenge to the country. Those who have an income and work to go to every day are less likely to be drawn into terrorist activity.[19]

In the Middle East, the *Palestine Centre for Rapprochement* has begun a long-term project aimed at providing teenagers in the Bethlehem area with a positive alternative to engaging in terrorism. Basketball is one of the most popular sports in the West Bank and the project co-ordinator, who is himself a basketball player and coach, provides the youngsters, both Christian and Muslim, with regular training sessions in the sport; he also arranges matches and socials at which the young people can meet in a friendly environment. In this way they can begin to see those of different religions and backgrounds as people rather than potential enemies.[20]

The Catholic Church has long sought to raise awareness of the close link between justice and peace. It therefore works for a more just society in every country, because, without justice, there can be no lasting peace. The purpose of the *Pontifical Council for Justice and Peace*, which was established in the late 1960s, is to promote a deeper understanding of the application of Gospel values to the practical problems in contemporary societies. The *Council* supports Justice and Peace work both at local and international level and it collaborates with organisations that support its aims, such as the (ecumenical) *World Council of Churches* and the UN.[21] Together, all these organisations offer hope for countries where the temptation to secure a better future through terrorist acts is greatest.

The Age of the Individual: Personal Responsibility

In our times, individuals, especially in the West, demand the right to control their lives as never before. The right to choose has become a watchword that is applied even to human life itself. This can be a positive development, if people choose to live by the objective truth; if they accept responsibility for the effect of their decisions on every human life involved.

However, many people claim a right to make choices which do not respect everyone's right to life. When that happens, the weakest and most defenceless in society are sacrificed for the sake of the presumed rights of the strongest. Duties to others, and to oneself, are overlooked in the general clamour for rights.

The claim that it is sometimes justifiable to destroy life for the sake of a desirable life is based on the untruth that the right to life does not apply equally to everyone. Those who base their lives on this claim may have an existence without pain, or rather, an anaesthetised life, but they will inevitably contribute to a society in which life is increasingly under threat and therefore dominated by fear. In such a society life cannot be good.

In order to create a good life for everyone, we all have a responsibility to seek the truth and live by it. This means that we have a duty to treat human life, not as a property to be disposed of, but as the gift from God that Christians believe it is.

The Ultimate Future: The Good Life for All

According to the Christian faith, the world as we know it will come to an end at the Second Coming of Christ, at the end of time. This is the ultimate future, the beginning of eternal life, which is meant for every man and woman. However, our life in eternity will depend on how we have lived during our lifetime. It will depend on whether we have included every human being in society, or whether we have sought a good life for ourselves by excluding or killing others, or by putting an end to our own lives.

The Second Coming of Christ is sometimes referred to as Judgement Day. It could also be called the Day of Truth, because it is the day on which the truth about each one of us will be revealed. The Gospel of St Matthew describes the basis on which our lives will be judged, which, surprisingly, does not depend on whether we knew or believed in Christ, but on how we treated our fellow human beings.

The evangelist speaks of the Last Judgement as the solemn occasion when Christ will gather all nations before him and divide them as a shepherd sorts sheep from goats.[22] He will separate those who have lived according to the mind of Christ from those who have not. He will invite the just to inherit the kingdom that has been prepared for them since the world began,

> For I was hungry and you gave me food,
> I was thirsty and you gave me drink,
> I was a stranger and you made me welcome, ...
> sick and you visited me.[23]

The just may then say to Christ that they did not know him and that they had never seen him in the plights which he describes. However, that is not what matters. The all-important thing is that they have acted in a compassionate way to the people in need that they came across and were able to help. Christ will tell them that, when they visited the sick or welcomed the stranger, they were in fact visiting or welcoming him, because every human being is created in the image and likeness of Christ.[24] He will say that what you did to the least of my brothers, you did to me: or, to put it differently, 'What you did to someone like John, the server at Mass, you did to me.'[25]

The welcoming of the stranger, the feeding of the hungry, and the visiting of the sick are particularly relevant to the questions about respect for human life that we have considered. The welcoming of the stranger applies both to the embryo and the unborn child, because the child conceived *in vitro* as well as the child in the womb are unknown human beings, until the time of birth; only then do they begin to be known to us. The welcoming of the stranger can also apply to the relationship between a particular community and a person from another country or culture with very different attitudes to those of the majority. In such a situation, those from the host country can try to make the person from the outside feel welcome and understood, thereby forestalling a temptation to terrorism.

The stipulation about visiting the sick includes meeting all their needs, in terms of medical care as well as nutrition. It means showing solidarity with them and respecting their lives, however handicapped or limited they are. It is incompatible with respect for someone's life to kill them or help them to kill themselves or to starve them to death by withdrawing food and drink.

The demand to care for the person in need who crosses our path is so fundamental that, according to the account of the Last Judgement, our eternal salvation depends on how we have responded to our neighbour in need or distress.

Forgiveness

This book has focused on the right to life of all without exception. Yet it is so generally assumed that there is a right to destroy human life, especially in connection with abortion and assisted suicide, that it is entirely possible someone reading this book might once have been involved in one of these practices. Later he or she might have come to the conclusion that what they did in the past was wrong. What then?

A person can only act according to what they know and understand at the time. The fact that they have come to realise that they would not now do what they once did is a sign of growth and of hope. It means that all is not lost.

Christ was and is always ready to forgive. Think of what he said to those who were crucifying him,

> Father, forgive them; they do not know what they are doing.[26]

The soldiers did not know that they were crucifying an innocent man. Many people involved in actions such as abortion and assisted suicide do not fully understand what they are doing. Therefore Christ's words are addressed to them too.

Whatever the situation, only God knows the mind of any particular person. Therefore, while the actions we have spoken of remain objectively wrong, no one has the right to condemn themselves or others for once having been involved in them.

Conclusion: The Good Life in Eternity

In our search for a good life, we have two options: We can seek to create it according to our own ideas, or we can decide to live the life that God has offered us and that is always waiting for us. If we choose to go our own way, we will end up destroying human beings in ever greater numbers in order to achieve an existence that is physically perfect and almost without pain. On the other hand, if we choose to accept life as a gift which we must cherish, then our lives may be hard, but they will also be good.

The examples from the recent past, from our own times and from fiction that we have looked at are warnings of what can happen, if a society seeks to create only perfect human beings, while excluding the imperfect. It is significant that the descriptions from literature of imaginary societies in which only some people are allowed to live, are all horror stories. They say something fundamental about our limitations, because we can destroy life, but, in spite of IVF, we cannot create it out of nothing.

Despair is the driving force behind all the destruction of human life that we have described, both from real life and from fiction: despair of a handicapped person being able to have a worthwhile existence, despair of being able to look after an unexpected child, despair of being able to care for a sick person. Where there is despair, fear is not far behind, because the only remedy for a perceived deficiency is death. On the other hand, hope makes it possible for us to believe that every life can be good, whatever the difficulties. Hope drives out fear and enables us to trust.

The alternative to the grim picture of life in a society where human beings are selectively destroyed is a community where everyone is included. This is the perfect life described in the *Book of Revelation*, when God will live among his people and there will be no more sorrow or suffering.[27]

We can begin to live like this, even during our time on earth, by accepting everyone, whether they are at the first stage of life or at the end. Only by respecting all humankind can we live a good life, because only then will we be living in truth.

Then we will never be able to say, 'Who is my neighbour?', because everyone is my neighbour, created by God and infinitely precious in his eyes.

Notes

[1]   A recent instance of this policy was referred to *in The Times* (27 June 2012).

[2]   H. Macdonald, *The Hummingbird Saint* (London: Michael Joseph, 2003) p. 222.

[3]   N. Gordimer, 'Reflections by Nobel Laureates' in Y. Danieli, E. Stamatopoulou and C. J. Dias, (eds.) *The Universal Declaration of Human Rights: Fifty Years and Beyond* (Amityville, NY: Baywood, 1998), as quoted in D. P. Forsythe, *Human Rights in International Relations* (Cambridge: Cambridge University Press, 2000), p. 39.

[4]   *Human Rights and Catholic Church*, Reflections on the Jubilee of the *Universal Declaration of Human Rights*, Catholic Bishop's Conference of England and Wales, (London: Catholic Media Office, 1998), 20.

[5]   Pope Benedict XVI, *Spe Salvi*, 37.

6   Pope Benedict XVI, *Spe Salvi*, 38.
7   *Ibid.*
8   Congregation for the Doctrine of the Faith, *Dignitas Personae*, 19.
9   As reported in *The Times*, 2 February 2006.
10   *Catechism of the Catholic Church*, 2376–2377.
11   Congregation for the Doctrine of the Faith, *Dignitas Personae*, 19.
12   http://www.careconfidential.com/WhatAboutAdoption.aspx . (2 July 2012).
13   Further information about these organisations can be found on their web sites: http://www.lifecharity.org.uk and http://www.careconfidential.com (2 July 2012).
14   http://www.crisispregnancyhelp.org/services.htm.
15   Pope Francis, *Amoris Laetitia*, 47.
16   See http://www.unicef.org/media/media_60790.html?q=printme (4 July 2012).
17   See http://www.larche.org.uk/about_idms.php.
18   A classic book on the subject is: M. Muggeridge, *Something Beautiful for God* (New York: HarperOne, 2003).
19   See https://www.gov.uk/government/case-studies/building-furniture-and-a-future-in-afghanistan (15 December 2015).
20   Fr P. Maddison, 'Basketball for Peace Project' in *Catholic East Anglia* (January 2016), p. 15.
21   For further information, see http://www.vatican.va/roman_curia/pontifical_councils/justpeace/index.htm .
22   Mt 25:31–32.
23   Mt 25:34–37.
24   Cf. Gn. 1:27.
25   Mt 25:40.
26   Lk 23:34.
27   Rev 21:4.

GLOSSARY

Aryan	A historical race concept which emerged in the period of the late 19th century and mid-20th century to describe people of Indo-European heritage as a racial grouping.
Aryanism	An ideology of racial supremacy which views the supposed Aryan race as a distinct and superior racial group entitled to rule the rest of humanity. Aryanism reached its peak of influence in Nazi Germany, where it was used to justify discrimination against minorities, which eventually culminated in the Holocaust.
Assisted suicide	Helping someone to kill themselves.
Blasphemy	The action or offence of speaking sacrilegiously about God.
Direct Action	Action such as civil disobedience with the aim of obtaining specific demands.
Ethical	In accordance with moral principles of conduct.

Eugenics	A method of improving the human race, especially by selective breeding.
Euthanasia	Literally 'easy death', killing someone to relieve suffering. Non-voluntary euthanasia involves killing someone without that person's consent, while voluntary euthanasia is carried out with the person's consent.
Hippocratic oath	Oath sworn by doctors, including a promise to respect life in all cases.
Hospice	A medical facility for the terminally ill, which enables them to live fully until they die.
IVF	In Vitro Fertilisation: fertilising an egg outside the body for later implantation.
Juridical Person	An entity, such as a firm, with a distinct identity and rights (Not a human being).
Living will	An advance directive about how to treat a sick person if he or she loses the ability to decide.
Mental capacity	Ability to think and make decisions.
Messiah	The redeemer expected by the Jews.
Objective (adj.)	Existing independently of personal opinion. The opposite of subjective.

Palliative care	Care of the terminally ill, which relieves pain and discomfort, while respecting life.
Promised Land	The land of Canaan, which God promised to Abraham and his descendants.
PVS state	Persistent Vegetative State: a wakeful, unresponsive state lasting longer than a few weeks.
Stem cell	An undifferentiated cell that gives rise to specialised cells.
Subjective (adj.)	Based on an individual's opinion. The opposite of objective.
Terrorism	The systematic use of violence and intimidation to achieve some goal. Frequently involves the taking of human life.
Third Reich	Official Nazi designation for the totalitarian regime in Germany from January 1933 to May 1945.

Lightning Source UK Ltd.
Milton Keynes UK
UKHW012319090320
360039UK00002B/45